Psychoframe is an expression I first started using in the late 1980s to describe the psychological frameworks I created for new supervisors at the Palmer Tube Mills steel plant to help them remember the basic principles of leadership and management. I later adapted the term for subsequent personal and business coaching programs in goal achievement, personal success and customer service.

Karel de Laat

About the Author

Karel de Laat completed his bachelor's and master's degrees in psychology and his doctorate in history in Australia. He worked as an organizational psychologist for more than thirty years, specializing in organization and career development. During this time he featured in newspapers and on radio, providing practical advice on how to achieve personal and business success, as well as presenting seminars on a wide range of business and career development subjects. In his spare time, Karel served in the Australian Naval Reserve for thirty years, attaining the rank of Rear-Admiral. He now devotes his time to writing, mentoring, consulting and public speaking. His other books include 'Hints for Personnel Success' and 'Business Tips.

About the Book

Personal Success Strategies is a guide to developing interpersonal skills that will make you more confident in interpersonal situations so that you will be able to achieve personal success. Personal success is defined as the ability to achieve what you want in life with an action philosophy that makes you happy, but also contributes to the world at a broader level. The guidance in this book is applicable to both personal and business/career situations. As an organizational psychologist, Karel de Laat has provided career and business advice to owners, managers and team members of large businesses for three decades. In his work, he collected numerous anecdotes and used them to motivate and guide his clients in the board room and in the heart of operations. Karel believes that everyone can attain personal and business success. They just have to know the right strategies. Karel's anecdotes and coaching guidelines show in a practical way how each of us can achieve personal and business success if we follow some very basic principles. These basic principles show us how to interact with others in a positive way, use our passion for our life goals to follow our unique path and how to do this in a courageous and sincere way.

.

A de Laat & Co book

Published by de Laat & Co
PO Box 9
Ferny Hills DC QLD Australia 4055
www.delaatco.com

© Frans Karel de Laat

First published 2014

Author: Karel de Laat
Title: Personal Success Strategies/Karel de Laat
ISBN 978 0 9872878 2 3
Subjects: psychology, philosophy

Personal Success Strategies

A Psychoframe for Life's Challenges

Karel de Laat

de Laat & Co

Contents

Preface

How to make the subject of being a success in life interesting and worth reading and talking about seems a strange challenge. You would think it would be pretty easy. Everybody would want to be successful wouldn't they? Unfortunately for all of us, it isn't that simple.

I suppose the challenge starts with the definition of success. It depends so much on your personal circumstances that defining success has more to do with the processes than the situation.

In writing my views on personal success for my radio program 'Hints for Personal Success', I noticed that the bulk of my examples came back to the interactions people were having every day. It was not so much about long-term planning as it was about the tools that let you enjoy life and move forward felling that you had done the best you could in each situation that you faced.

As I started to put everything together for this more permanent learning guide, I realised that my definition of success needed to be practical because it needed to be immediately useful if it was to catch anyone's imagination and help them on a long term basis.

In getting help from a range of people to see how the ideas would be used, I realised that only one thing needed to be changed in many peoples' lives for the ideas to be useful. To expect more was unrealistic, because there was just too much happening to everybody. In fact, the simpler I could make it the better it would be.

I have always said to the people I have coached, that if you can grasp firmly just the one thing that you want at the time, and make it happen, you will have achieved a change that will bring you the feeling of success.

This book is about identifying that one thing, doing it, feeling what success is and moving on with a new view of your life and what success means to you.

Most importantly, success is what you decide it should be not what anyone else tells you. In a world that is increasingly complex and where social pressure from a variety of media has you under so much pressure, the key to success is to remain grounded in your own reality. Personal Success Strategies aims to help you find that reality. I hope it helps.

Best wishes,

Karel de Laat

Chapter1

How it all started

Introduction

Ideas for personal success are easy to generate and access. You can read about them in the media every day. The trouble is that they have very limited long term application unless they are focused on what you want.

Having been asked how to make the ideas from my book 'Hints for Personal Success' a long term change strategy I decided to use material from my consulting work to produce Practical Success Strategies.

Personal Success Strategies takes the reverse approach to Hints for Personal Success and other books based on miscellaneous ideas from case studies. Personal Success Strategies starts off by getting you to define your personal success ideas before looking in more detail at what you can do about it.

The psychology and philosophy of Personal Success Strategies is based on the principle that your personal success belongs to you and no one else. Further, the saying that comparisons are odious, so that they contribute more to failure than they do to success, is one of the smartest things ever said.

This book is really a simple personal instruction guide for exploring your personal success. In the first few chapters, I explain what I believe success is, and what it is not. I then spend the rest of the book letting you explore what it means to you and deciding how to use the approach I present to achieve your view of personal success.

The key to using the ideas in Personal Success Strategies is having a go without fear. It is a bit of a funny thing that Personal Success Strategies has the goal of helping you get rid of your personal demons, but before you can really use it you have to work on your own to at least say what those demons are. The good thing is that by reading this far you have probably already decided to do that anyway.

Try to have fun with the ideas, no matter how serious your issues, because you will be guided by your best friend, the person that understands you best and the person that will get most out of everything good that happens - you. If you and your inner self get together to explore Personal Success Strategies, you can stick together to achieve whatever you want.

Without boring you with too much detail, I need you to understand that Personal Success Strategies is a behaviour or action learning system with a variety of psychological principles behind it. The most basic one is that you can manage any aspect of your life if you have an understandable and manageable system for dealing with what happens to you. This of course is much easier said than done.

There is a lot more personal success and happiness literature that you can read to develop your skills and the Personal Success Strategies approach does not involve any secret mumbo jumbo that locks you into anything. It does work, however, on the principle that you can do a lot for yourself with just some basic ideas and a determination to be happy and successful (whatever that means to you). So, enough theory, let's get on with the business of considering the principles and techniques that I would like you to learn and use. Remember though, this is all about you, so consider the questionnaires and sample answers as a mirror of what you think now and would like to review.

The material is not intended to shine a light that you follow blindly. You must remain in charge of the process as it is intended that the process will help you take charge of and remain in charge of all aspects of what you do so that you can live a happy and fulfilling live on a day to day basis.

Overview

Let me begin with a few words of warning. Personal Success Strategies is about learning new social skills to improve how you manage interpersonal situations. It is not a substitute for situations where counseling is required. So, if you are looking for help because you are not coping socially, then this book may help, but you need to be sure that there is no other issue that needs the attention of a health care professional.

Some years ago I was given the task of training all employees at a remote facility, because the head of the facility was a bully. He was a very capable technician in an unusual discipline, no replacement could be found because of the remote location and he had been there a long time. In addition, his bullying was always focused on the very high technical standards he set and his view that various members of the team were unable to meet these very high standards.

This disagreement on performance standards had not been resolved by a range of measure introduced by the corporate human resources specialists and I was brought in to try to find a solution. What I found was a team that respected the head technician's ability but had a lot of problems with his poor interpersonal skills.

I had been told that the head technician had been counseled on repeated occasions, but that he stood by his view that his demand for exemplary performance in such a high risk environment was perfectly reasonable. The reality was that the environment was very high risk and previous discussions had become bogged down when the head technician asked senior management if they wanted him to take a more lenient approach even if this meant a great risk of system failure and potentially fatal results. The answer was always – no.

With this stalemate in place, I was asked to work with the staff to consider what options there were for improving the situation.

After a number of team meetings, I concluded that the team believed that the bullying did not come from the head technician's desire to be nasty, but from a genuine desire to do the work perfectly in a way consistent with the high risk processes involved. There was also an element of conceit about his ability, however, that made the head technician a 'pain' to work with.

When I presented the choice between the current head technician and one that was more pleasant, but less competent, all team members said the competence level was the number one issue. It had to be, they all agreed, because errors had fatal consequences.

This is probably the best time to note that some team members had no problems with the head technician. They saw him as a pain with an unfortunate manner, but they did not take it personally and focused on the technical demands. Conversely, the head technician identified these people who were unaffected by his poor interpersonal skills as competent or reasonably good at their jobs. These people were the clue to one possible strategy.

Thus, I was in a situation where some team members did not see the head technician as a bully to everyone, a not unusual situation. In addition, these more competent and confident team members even canvassed the idea that it was the inability of some team members to cope with the high standards required that was creating their stress, not the manner of the supervisor.

At this point I formulated an approach based on teaching affirmative action skills to those team members who could not 'manage' the supervisor and felt that they needed these additional skills. This focused on the broader idea of defining their needs in a work role and what skills would help them meet these needs.

Before taking any action I also had a comprehensive and very frank discussion with the supervisor about the quality of the people he was alienating and, in some cases, intimidating by his hard stance. Not surprisingly, to me anyway, he was genuinely surprised at the impact of his attitude and some of the people he was affecting the most were those he held in the highest regard. There were others for whom he had very low regard, but could not replace for a variety of reasons. As with all human relationship challenges, this assignment was not going to be simple.

The Psychoframe process that resulted is what I will explain to you now. All the staff at the facility completed the program and began to understand how they could take charge of their interactions with the supervisor. Strangely, the end behaviors of the team were not that dissimilar to those of the supervisor.

The details of the system I developed are the subject of this book. After I completed this assignment I found the methodology useful in other parts of the cooperate sector and then started to apply it in individual coaching. In the rest of this chapter I will provide a philosophical overview and then the remainder of the book is designed to allow you to use the tools and philosophies to understand the basic framework and apply it to your needs.

The starting point for any change is to understand the current situation or circumstances. In this situation, doing a personal review is the key to moving forward as it lets you define where you are now and how far that is away from where you want to be.

The program begins by assessing where you are up to in your goal of a happy and fulfilling life and as you progress through the book you discover what your answers mean and what you can do about it. It is a process of self discovery fully managed by you as your own best friend. You may wish to share some thoughts with others, but I suggest you consider if this indicates a need for professional input.

A further word of warning

At the beginning of the learning process, a Personal Review Form (PRF) and a Personal Success (PSQ) are used to assess your training needs. If you complete these forms and feel you are not ready to do the training program because you have personal issues you cannot resolve without individual counseling, you should take the very positive and worthwhile step of seeing a qualified counselor.

How the program works

Personal Success Strategies is based on the principle that you will perform better in social situations if you understand what is happening and are prepared.

The Program teaches a structure for analysing social situations and choosing the best strategy to achieve personal success, which is basically defined as coping with **most** social situations in a way that leaves you feeling relaxed and satisfied about yourself and your place in the world. I say most, because we all will be embarrassed and lost for words at sometime. Nobody is perfect and we just want a good overall result in most situations.

For long term personal success, the program uses training to improve your ability to manage a wide range of social situations.

What you have to do

Any behaviour change requires an understanding and acceptance of the principles involved plus motivation to make the effort to acquire and apply the necessary skills.

To acquire the skills, you have to learn the principles and practice the skills.

How does the Personal Success Questionnaire (PSQ) work?

The principles that lead to personal success in most social situations can be learned and your improvement can be assessed on the PSQ. The skills can be practiced alone using mental rehearsal (which is a valuable tool for preparing for all interactions), but personal success occurs when the skills are applied in everyday life. The PSQ can be used repeatedly to assess your level of knowledge of the principles required. There is a flow on acceptance of the principles because you have committed yourself to learning and using what the program teaches.

Your level of knowledge and acceptance of the Personal Success Principles is the platform from which you launch yourself. The more thoroughly you learn the principles and understand and accept the appropriateness of the program and its contents for your needs, the higher the likelihood of success.

How Permanent Will Any Change In Behavior Be?

Experience with people who have completed Personal Success Strategies indicates that immediate success in certain areas is not difficult to attain. Also, longer term improvements in overall feelings of social competence and confidence have been reported for a wide variety of needs.

The aim of Personal Success Strategies is to give you the skill to manage your life with purpose, confidence, and a range of social skills that leaves you feeling fulfilled and achieving what is generally referred to as personal success.

The concept of personal success is one that has had many interpretations. Material success has been prominent because it is unequivocal evidence of having succeeded in accumulating things. Personal success is the opposite of this concept because it is measured by accumulating experiences.

Do I have to keep practicing the principles?

Of course! Personal success is a way of life and requires you to use the principles in every situation to achieve the fulfillment that you are seeking in both the mental and physical aspects of life.

You may choose to stop at a certain point when you feel you have achieved as much as you want, but you will still need to use the principles to maintain your level of improvement.

This basic overview of Personal Success Strategies was intended to give you a clear understanding of what the process will and will not do for you. It is a stepping off point to make sure you realize that there is no magic in any program, only a tool that you choose to use to help you to get you where you want to go.

There are detailed instructions for every part of the process that follows, but if you are unsure of the general process you should read the overview again. Also, feel free to come back to it at any time during the process.

Notes for my personal success plan

CHAPTER 2

Reviewing Your Life

Introduction

Something we all do a lot is look at where we are and where we have been. We also look at the people we know and how have they moved on in comparison to ourselves. Personal Success Strategies is very big on self-pacing and supports developing the view that 'comparisons are odious' as a healthy approach to life. In other words, you have one life to lead and that is the one you should concentrate on.

Some of the following ideas are central to the concepts in Personal Success Strategies.

You pace yourself, but you set the pace.

There is no correct formula for how a life is lived.

You can achieve anything you want to, just don't do it at other peoples' expense.

Having a strategy is not complicated. It just means you thought about what you wanted to do with your life.

Personal Success Strategies asks questions of you and then gives examples of how other people have answered some of these questions – for them not you.

You may choose to never share your answers to the various questions, which is fine. If you are happy that you have understood the question and made a commitment to yourself to think about what it means to you are on your way to setting your pace, with your personal formula, so that you set your goals and prepare your strategies for having a successful life

Reviewing where you are up to and where you want to go

The Personal Review Form below allows you to set the guidelines within which you will use your Personal Success Strategies to discover how to achieve what you want out of life.

PERSONAL REVIEW FORM (PRF)

Name: _____ **Date:** _____

PERSONAL DEVELOPMENT

Question: What areas of your life do you want to improve?

Answer:

_____
_____
_____
_____
_____
_____
_____
_____
_____
_____
_____
_____
_____
_____
_____
_____
_____
_____

PERSONAL HISTORY

Question: How long have you been working on the personal development issues that are the greatest challenge for you?

Answer:

_____

Question: What have you done up to now to achieve your personal development goals?

Answer:

_____
_____
_____
_____
_____
_____
_____
_____
_____
_____
_____
_____
_____
_____
_____
_____
_____
_____
_____
_____
_____
_____

ACHIEVEMENT EXPECTATIONS

Question: How long do you expect it will take before you start to make satisfactory progress on the achievement of your personal development goals?

Answer:

YOUR DEVELOPMENT STRATEGY

Question: What current plans or ideas do you think are most likely to help you achieve your personal development goals?

Answer:

CRITICAL FACTORS

List all the information that you think is relevant to the achievement of your personal development goals. (How problems arose etc).

_____
_____
_____
_____
_____
_____
_____
_____
_____
_____
_____
_____
_____
_____
_____
_____
_____
_____
_____
_____
_____
_____

Now that you have summarized the most important information that relates to the achievement of your personal success goals, you can develop a plan to get where you want to go. The abilities to make this plan work are the subject of the remaining chapters of the book. Personal success skills are finite abilities and the aim of Personal Success Strategies is the learning of the skills needed to make the achievement of your goals a structured and controlled process that you can apply whenever and wherever you choose.

CHAPTER 3

Personal Success Strategies

Introduction

The development of the behaviors you need to interact positively and successfully with others in a personally rewarding way is no different than learning any other skill.

The Personal Success Questionnaire (PSQ) which follows is a progressive assessment learning tool. You can use the PSQ to assess your current strategies for dealing with social situations, re-program your behavior to suit the goals you want to achieve and re-test yourself with the PSQ to measure the quantity and quality of your new behaviors.

On the first run through, you answer the questions using completely honest responses that represent how you currently behave. This allows you to determine your current strategies, so that when you re-use the PSQ to assess your progress in learning new skills, you get a true comparison against the 'old' you.

Trying hard to think of what you would like to do and writing that response defeats the purpose of the initial use of the PSQ, because it gives a falsely positive view of how socially competent you are.

You should answer the PSQ now in a way that provides a base line to determine a starting off point for new behaviors that you will develop as you work through the material in the book.

Just answer the questions naturally as thought you were in that situation right now, talking to someone. You do not have to share you work with anyone as this is a self pacing process. Finally, try to have fun with it as one of the first steps in making your personnel success a daily part of your life.

PERSONAL SUCCESS QUESTIONNAIRE (PSQ)

Name: _____ Date: _____

INSTRUCTIONS

The PSQ is designed to help you learn more about your approach to personal challenges. It is open-ended and requires written answers.

The PSQ contains a series of statements followed by a space for you to write your response. You are required to respond as if you were speaking to someone who may make a statement or ask a question. Your response should be about **your** attitudes, beliefs and experiences. You should not respond with a question.

Do not worry if you have no experience in this area. The PSQ uses no special jargon or other expressions which would be unfamiliar to you. Alternatively, although the questions are intended to be general, you may feel happier answering in relation to a particular situation you have experienced. Feel free to use any method of approach.

The aim is to allow you to give your views on a variety of issues by simulating a discussion.

HERE IS A SAMPLE OF WHAT YOU WILL BE REQUIRED TO DO

Statement: Personal development training seems so vague.

Response: Not if I focus on specific things and practice key behaviors.

PSQ Instructions (continued)

You may write as much as you like in the space provided, but you need to make **only two** different points to complete the item and achieve the maximum score of two points.

The PSQ is completed with a time limit because the situations which are simulated are usually done under pressure with no opportunity to correct errors made.

You will have 30 minutes to do as many of the questions as possible. Work **quickly** but not so fast that you make mistakes. Are you ready?

Please turn over and start work.

PERSONAL SUCCESS QUESTIONNAIRE

1.   Statement: How are you feeling today?

     Responses:

1_____

2_____

2.   Statement: I just can't seem to get enthusiastic about anything.

     Response:

1_____

2_____

3.   Statement: What is independent thinking about anyway?

     Response:

1_____

2_____

4.   Statement: What is courage?

     Response:

1_____

2_____

5.   Statement: What is sincerity?

     Response:

1_____

2_____

6.   Statement: Do you get depressed sometimes?

      Response:
1_____

2_____

7.   Statement: Does being intense about things tire you
out?

      Response:
1_____

2_____

8.   Statement: Does being independent-minded mean you
are a loner?

      Response:
1_____

2_____

9.   Statement: How is courage relevant to personal
success?

      Response:
1_____

2_____

10.   Statement: Why will people accept what I say?

      Response:
1_____

2_____

11. Statement: You can't help feeling bad, if everyone around you feels bad.

Response

1_____

2_____

12. Statement: I don't like to get involved.

Response:

1_____

2_____

13. Statement: So what do I get out of developing independent-mindedness?

Response:

1_____

2_____

14. Statement: How do I learn to be courageous?

Response:

1_____

2_____

15. Statement: What is the key to success in personal relationships?

Response:

1_____

2_____

16.   Statement: Negative people are more powerful than positive people.

Response:

1_____

2_____

17.   Statement: Being intense just isn't me!

Response:

1_____

2_____

18.   Statement: Does being independent-minded mean you rebel against everything?

Response:

1_____

2_____

19.   Statement: How do I face someone that I've always been scared of?

Response:

1_____

2_____

20.   Statement: Isn't being genuine a bit of a weak strategy?

Response:

1_____

2_____

21. Statement: It's easier to be negative than positive!

     Response:

1 _____

2 _____

22. Statement: What's the point of getting passionate about things?

     Response:

1 _____

2 _____

23. Statement: How do I know if I'm independent-minded?

     Response:

1 _____

2 _____

24. Statement: Does success behavior get easier?

     Response:

1 _____

2 _____

25. Statement: I'd rather just keep people at a distance!

     Response:

1 _____

2 _____

So what do i do now?

The answers to the PSQ will become self evident as you read the Personal Success Strategies that follow. You will use the strategies to check the answers you have given and shape new answers which will form the basis of your future behavior.

The new behaviors you choose may be in this book but they may also be in other books or sources that form part of your learning experience. Similarly, you may be very happy with your responses, which may or may not align with the Personal Success Strategies in this book. This is just one frame of reference to use as part of your search for your personal success in life.

Before moving to the next chapter where we will consider the five basic personal success behaviors that are measured in the PSQ, let's have a look at a few instances of interpersonal interactions and how they relate to these personal success characteristics and the PSQ.

The five characteristics are

1. **Positive**
2. **Intense**
3. **Independent-minded**
4. **Courageous**
5. **Sincere**

As an example, how do you make personal success happen now by being more **positive**? It's simple. First, every day when you are asked 'How are you?'. From this moment forward you have to resolve to say that you are 'terrific, great, never been better'. Saying so makes that your goal and your goal turns into reality when you interpret your view of the universe from a positive perspective, regardless of the circumstances. This aspect of personal success strategies is not new and there are innumerable books on the subject.[1]

---

[1] Positive thinking has been around for thousands of years, but is probably best explored in writings on Zen Buddhism.

When it's second nature for you to say that you feel great, one reason you will feel better and more able to cope is because, by increasing your level of arousal, your ability to succeed increases through having more energy and a greater attention span.

This is why positive thinking works. It is not magical. It is purely that you make a choice to take a positive approach and this becomes your reality long enough for you to implement the best strategy to solve the real problems that confront you.[2]

Consequently, you do succeed, or feel that you have done the best you can, and you feel happy with what you have done. Your expectation becomes real and the best part is that it stays real because being happy is an enjoyable habit just like being miserable is a not at all an enjoyable habit.

So start right now, step one in making success happen is to automatically say when someone says 'How are you?', 'I am terrific, I've never felt better'. Practice it, right now and get used to using the words, just the way you would write them as a response to Question 1 on the PSQ. It is also important to realize that when you say 'terrific' or 'great' or whatever suits you, that it is you who determines how positive thinking strategy is used. You are on the way, because you are choosing your own behavior.

Similarly, to be **intense** you've got to enjoy and be committed to what you do and that is as simple as saying, 'Isn't this great'. You will challenge other people with your enthusiasm and your intensity about what you are doing, so practice those words with whatever you are doing, 'Isn't this great'.

Invariably, people will challenge you. This is exactly what you want because your personal success comes from your ability to manage your thoughts and overcome negatives.

---

[2] Read more about arousal, attention and the need for achievement in basic academic texts in psychology.

When you say, 'Isn't this great' and someone looks at you as though you are crazy and it doesn't affect you at all, you know that you are well on your way with your personal success strategy. Actually what will happen is that people will say to you 'What's got into you?' because they will want to feel the same.

In the next chapter, I will look at some general examples of success, but you need to keep yourself focused on what you want and relate everything I say back to you and what you wrote in the PRF and PSQ. All the theory and examples might be interesting and have a little bit of a general learning effect, but to really make a difference you want to keep it all as personal as you can.

There is a reason horoscopes and fantasy literature remain so popular despite the communication revolution making the harsh realities of life so clear. We do not want to let go of the idea that there is something magical 'out there' that relieves us of the burden of having to decide about life and how it should be lived.[3]

---

[3] Numerous books have been written on how humans decide things emotionally and rationalize their decisions logically.

CHAPTER 4

Key Issues

In this chapter I talk about the background to the PRF and PSQ and how you use them in real life. Now is a good time to start making notes, as you go, on the Personal Action List (PAL) at the end of the book (if you think I am having fun making up all these abbreviations, then you are right).

The PAL is based on the Personal Success Strategies principles and is designed to focus your effort on the things that matter most to you. Feel free to jump around on the PAL as the mood takes you. The rule for your PAL is that you make the rules so you enjoy the game (of life). At the end of each chapter, which discusses a personal success strategy, I have included a PAL as well.

Now let's get on with some scenarios that I hope you will find familiar and be able to translate into working examples for you. They are supposed to be as simple and realistic as possible because that is what life is supposed to be like - simply, easy and fun.

I have purposely not filled the book with references and ways to justify what I say, because I want you to form your own opinion, not agree with something because I refer to some higher authority. Not wanting to live your life on the basis of what someone else says or thinks is probably the reason you are reading this in the first place. Here you are the authority on what is important. I am just presenting you with some thoughts and (hopefully) options that keep emphasizing the central role of your thoughts and actions in approaching life's challenges how this will determine how successful you will be in finding happiness and contentment.

What is success?

Having spoken so much about personal success to this point, but also using words like happiness and contentment, I thought it might be appropriate to revisit what personal success really means.

I have said before that it is definitely not limited to factors associated with money or power or any of the other issues that I am sure so many people have used to define success in their minds.

Personal success is not a narrow concept. It operates across a broad band where peoples' wants and needs are matched against their efforts to achieve their goals. The important thing about this very general definition of personal success is that the assessment of achievement is individual. It is not a comparison of you against other people. It is an issue of you comparing your achievements against the standards you have set for yourself.

For this reason, personal success, and the happiness and contentment that goes with it, can be achieved by everyone at their own level.

It is extremely important, but difficult, to understand that the personal happiness and contentment that you achieve is equally fulfilling to that achieved by the great people in history, they just happened to get more publicity.

The examples that I use now and in later chapters on the personal various success strategies are intended to emphasize that it is how you think, what you do and how you do it that brings about true personal success. Nothing magical in that is there. But it is amazing how few people actually stop to think about how they can shape their thinking and behavior to have a more enjoyable life.

Be aware of different perspectives

One very important life lesson for all of us is acquiring an awareness of the different perspectives held by other people. It is very common to make the mistake of believing that other people view the world exactly as we do, particularly in areas such as honesty, reliability and so on. This is not so.

Life is about differences and there is a wide range of perspectives that are very different to yours. In some cases, other peoples' views, and the actions that follow, may not fall outside the law, but will certainly fall outside of what you might regard as appropriate.

Someone who adopts a successful approach to life does not take these different perspectives to heart, and become bitter, but is certainly aware that their perspectives on honesty, reliability and similar characteristics, that form that essence called 'character', are not shared by each and every individual that they meet

The key to being successful is keeping this difference in perspectives clearly in your mind.. If you do this you can deal with people on their merits, make your own decisions about how other peoples' perspectives fit with your own, or not, and then make decisions about potential personal and working relationships accordingly.

Without developing a cynical view about having to sit constantly in judgment upon others, it's very advisable on the trail to success to ensure early in the piece that you are dealing with people who are like minded. This will keep you clear of those people who will cause you grief by maintaining and acting upon beliefs that you are not happy with.

Great minds think alike they say, but minds that think alike have a greater chance at success as well.

Be recognized

One of the key survival strategies for being successful in life is recognizing the importance of striking a balance between what is and what *seems* to be, between achieving and being *seen* to achieve, between perception and reality, between presentation and substance or, as is so much more commonly said:

Be aware of the difference between bull dust and brains and recognize the importance of each.

These may seem like harsh words but I can give you an example of a very senior successful person who was concerned who was plagued by person doubt in this area.

He sought my advice because, while he had been successful, other people that he worked alongside for years (and he knew to be far less competent than him) were just as successful because they were able to present a good image and (as he put it), always fool people for just long enough to get the next good job.

The key to being successful is to make sure that you don't become bitter and disillusioned because you don't have the skill to use the right blend of presentation and performance or the ability to work with perception as well as reality to achieve your goals. Stand up and make sure you are recognized for what you do.

Will this cure what my colleague saw as the major problem of less competent executive bluffing their way into good jobs. No, it won't, but it will mean that those who are competent are not overlooked and they may even be in the situation to address poor outcomes from poor decisions by their less competent colleagues.

Communicate at an appropriate level

Sometimes people have criticized me for changing my way of communicating depending on who I am speaking to.

My view has always been that you *should* change your style of interacting and presentation to suit the circumstances, particularly if you wish to gain acceptance. Also, it is common courtesy not to embarrass or alienate your hosts, friends or even complete strangers by not responding appropriately to the social requirements of a situation.

A very important part of being successful in life is to make people feel comfortable by dressing, speaking and acting in a way that is appropriate for the circumstances. You do not have to do anything elaborate in these areas. It may be as simple as wearing business clothing or being casually dressed when the situation requires.

Similarly, it is a situation of discussing matters that are suitable in the circumstances. It may be most appropriate not to speak about any other than light subjects or, on the other hand, it may be more appropriate to speak about challenging matters such as politics and mainstream social change issues.

Whatever the situation, it is merely a question of listening and interpreting the demands on the day. This is not difficult but can pay very significant dividends.

Relationships

One of the major difficulties people have in being personally successful is in developing good relationships. In my view success in this area comes from developing the capacity to be honest with other people by reducing your fear of how they will react.

Most people tend to disguise or alter their presentation and feelings about a situation because they fear how the other person will react. The goal should be to be fully open and positive with people not matter how difficult the circumstances. To be successful in this area it is important to do two things.

First, it is necessary to present your own impressions, feelings and desires in a straightforward and unemotional way. Clearly this is not easy, but starting with more simple situations will give you some opportunity to develop the skill. Second, it is important to understand and learn to cope with other peoples' reactions to an honest presentation of your feelings.

I believe this area merits a 'proceed with caution' warning. Do not blurt out your feelings at the first opportunity. Work with very simple and unthreatening feelings until you develop the skill to ensure that the outcome is generally positive for both parties. Managed correctly, it should be very positive indeed, but managed poorly it can be disastrous, so **PROCEED WITH CAUTION**.

Feet of clay stay that way

It has always surprised me how many people are overwhelmed, intimidated, daunted or in awe of academic or other qualifications.

Respect and reward for ability is certainly very positive and we should do everything that we can to promote achievement in ourselves and in others. However, having unrealistic expectations or perceptions of other individuals because of the position they hold, or the qualifications they have gained, can be quite dangerous.

All that obtaining a qualification proves is that the person is able to obtain qualifications, pass exams or whatever. Any further conclusions that one draws about people must be balanced by a close examination of what skill they have demonstrated beyond the most basic qualification.

As much as some people might like to convince us otherwise, all people are different. They will always have different levels of skill. The differences may be minute on occasions, but mostly they are not. So while the title may say soldier, sailor or candlestick maker, do not expect to get the same defense, safe passage or quality of trade work from different people with the same title.

There is some comfort in knowing that the longer the period of training, such as in medicine, the more likely it will be that you receive consistency in quality of service. Successful people, however, still choose their service providers based on knowledge of their ability, not a piece of paper.

Get the right advice

We all like to buy the best. One of the problems with being constantly barraged with advertising is that there can be a reaction against doing what is the best thing to achieve success.

One particularly important example is personal investment. A friend told me recently where, by getting professional advice, he was able to get a much better return on his savings than had been the case up to that point in time.

Don't worry about being barraged with advertising, it's an essential part of knowing what's available, so that you can go out and make the best choice.

As with so many other things, however, the best referral is a personal one. Usually this is brought about by you knowing that the particular adviser you choose has been successful in advising someone else that you trust and respect.

If you do not do this sort of reference checking, then you are just gambling on the providers own opinion about themselves and very few people in the selling business have a poor opinion about their products and services.

So if you want to be successful, in wealth creation for example, get the right advice from someone that you know has created wealth for someone else that you respect as a self manager and decision maker - but don't fool yourself, the decision must be made by you.

Go for perfection in something

One thing that I think that is most notable about people who achieve success is their fascination with achieving perfection in at least one thing.

No matter how obscure it may be, successful people seem to choose to explore the limits of their abilities by trying to be the best or close to the best in a certain area.

Interestingly, this greatest passion may not necessarily relate directly to their efforts to be personally successful, whether it is in work achievement, accumulation of wealth, and so on.

\   Nevertheless, this passion provides a perspective on what it means to achieve at the highest possible level. This perspective on the pursuit of perfection then flows to other areas of their life.

Too often we think of the elements that make up a perfect performance only in terms of the rarest individuals in the world. In reality, we should all work to find an interest where we can strive for perfection. What may seem like a very minor achievement need not be less perfect than one that changes the world

The beauty of striving and succeeding in this way is the total personal experience of fulfillment, on the one hand, and the flow on in terms of personal perspective with all other activities, on the other hand, that I mentioned earlier.

So whatever your passion live it to the full as it can have an amazingly broad and meaningful impact on your life and lead you to greater success in other areas, as well as being intrinsically rewarding.

Physical fitness

There has been an encouraging trend for people generally to be more fit. Certainly, there has been a strong trend towards taking early morning walks on a daily basis. I mentioned this because it is a safe and inexpensive way of staying in good physical shape.

Also, there is a lot of support for the view that a moderate amount of physical exercise is beneficial for everyone. The key issue is how to fit the appropriate exercise into a successful lifestyle.

Some people prefer to walk early in the morning while others prefer to get involved with team sports. The attractiveness of the exercise is important as it should motivate you to exercise every day or three or four times a week.

The successful person will find a form of exercise that suits their needs physically and suits their temperament. Even some of the greatest champions have indicated that certain forms of exercise, which would be beneficial for their overall development, are just so boring that they do not persist with them.

So, if you do attempt some form of physical fitness program, don't give up if the first effort is not rewarded. Look at other options and give other types of exercise a try. It is very likely you will find something that suits your schedule and your needs.

No matter what you find to be suitable to your needs and talents, the rewards will definitely be there in improved physical health and mental alertness.

Relaxation

One of the skills that eludes many people is the ability to relax. Yes it is a skill.

It is very simple really and requires no more than finding the time and place just to have a lie down and close your eyes.

It can't be that simple you say, but think about it. How often do you make the opportunity just to get away from it all? When did you take a break for the express purpose of relaxing?

The aim is to put yourself outside the mental and physical environment that creates stress. This can be done most successfully by physically removing yourself to a nearby park or other restful area, but this is often not possible. Sometimes you cannot even find a place to lie down, but you can still use your mind to pursue peace.

Even sitting quietly with your eyes gently closed can be enough to get you started. In fact you have probably seen people on public transport sitting like this for an entire journey. They may be sleeping, but often they are just in a state of pure relaxation. The trick is to be able to put your worries out of your mind.

When you are lying down or sitting in a relaxed way, you can increase your relaxation by several simple techniques such as taking a few slow deep breaths and imagining yourself to be in a setting that you find totally relaxing.

It may be at the beach or in the country, but it has to be a scene that makes you feel totally secure. The trick is to use your imagination to the point where you can feel the cool country breeze or hear the sound of the waves lapping on the shore.

So make that five minutes or ten minutes to relax. You will be surprised how easy it is to at least partially recharge your batteries. The best part of this process is that it gets better with practice. If you really like it, you may want to explore some of the many classes available in mediation.

Use your strengths, improve your weaknesses

For many years, personal improvement strategists have preached the merits of listing your strengths and weaknesses. This can be a very sound philosophy, but it must be approached in the right way.

If you list your strengths and weaknesses and are able to concentrate on the strengths, in the first instance, you can give yourself a sound base to work from. This puts you on the right track.

If you adopt the reverse philosophy, however, and develop an unhealthy emphasis on your weaknesses, and forget about your strengths, you can be in real trouble.

I favor listing as many strengths as you can, but only identifying one particular weakness that you would like to work on and making it one that you feel is particularly susceptible to intervention at the time.

In this way you give yourself a better chance of maintaining a positive base to work from as well as having an achievable goal for improving a particular area of weakness.

Somehow, having those strengths on your side makes looking at a weakness less daunting and success that much more achievable.

How far do you want to go?

Having spent my life assessing other people and attempting to help them realize their potential, one of the things that is most important to me is to help people understand that their rewards are adjusted according to the circumstances that they live in.

Simply put, it is just as easy for an individual living a 'normal' life to feel pain and pleasure at the same level as individuals that may appear to be living in much more privileged circumstances.

I call this phenomenon the 'Layers of Life Principle'. The Layers of Life Principle is most relevant when you consider your personal rewards and how they will affect you, permanently or temporarily.

As an example, if we equate the Layers of Life arbitrarily with income (and I say arbitrarily because I don't want to be seen to equate success with money alone), the middle layers represent most of us (by definition).

As average people we are always ebbing and flowing in terms of our ability to meet our financial commitments. We spend a bit too much, we save a little bit, we save a little bit more and then we spend too much again. Sound familiar?

Throughout our lives, most of us are slowly rising through several layers to the point where we eventually retire and probably then drop back a layer or two in terms of the amount of money we have available to spend. This particular pattern of rising through the various layers of life is normal.

What is crucial to success is the understanding of just how far you want to go. When you have set your goals and achieved them - *be happy.* Do not look sideways and judge your life by what others have done.

The Layers of Life Principle also embodies the essence of shaping what you are thinking so that you focus on personal successes in your day to day interactions.

Once again, there is no magic. Personal success comes from a very basic understanding of what you want out of life and how to get what you want.

In the chapters that follow think about how this applies to what happens to you on a daily basis. After each section explaining the principle, I will give applications of the principle in terms of the day to day interactions that happen to all of us.

CHAPTER 5

Positive Behavior

Now that we have looked at a few examples of common challenges, we can start looking in more detail at what the PSQ measured and how it relates to what you want out of life. Please don't be put off by the small amount of theory and teaching material that appears in each chapter. I will try to keep everything simple and (hopefully) interesting and relevant.

A bit of simple theory

How you act has an effect on how you feel.

Positive behavior gives the pleasure of discharging stored energy through achievement, and achievement leaves you with an after taste of satisfaction and self respect.

Negative behavior, on the other hand, gives the pleasure of discharging stored energy through escape, but escape leaves you with an after taste of frustration and a lack of self respect.

For example, think of the classic situation of someone who has a fear of someone intruding into their home. They check the windows and doors every half-hour. Every time they check they feel some relief for the first 15 minutes, but then for the next 15 minutes the tension builds up to the point where they just have to check the windows and doors again.

They know they are locked, but they cannot help themselves. Each time they check the house, they feel relief. However, they hate themselves for being so weak and are frustrated at the chain of events which locks them into this syndrome.

Most importantly, they know could turn this situation around if only they could control their thoughts. So how can you start to control your thoughts?[4]

The process I will now describe is broken up into definitions, action words and behaviors.

Definition: The policy of deliberately choosing 'feel good' thoughts (attitudes) as opposed to 'feel bad' thoughts.

Statements to use: I feel wonderful, great and so on.

Action:

1. Whenever you are asked, always say 'I feel wonderful, great, or whatever positive statement is natural for you.

2. When a negative mood strikes you, use music or positive self talk to change to a positive mood.

3. List the people close to you who support you and make you feel good about yourself.

4. Spend a whole day seeking and accepting only positive ideas, words and images while 'mentally marking' the negatives with a big black cross.

Look at the following examples and think about how they apply to you. There is a Personal Action List (PAL) at the end of this chapter for notes on what you are thinking and how you can be more positive.

---

[4] I may sound like I am being overly cautious here, but I must remind you that if you have any behaviour problems that interfere unduly in your daily home or work routine to the point where you cannot cope, you need to seek professional help.

You are your own image

There is a lot of talk in the area of personal development training about being only as successful as you dream you can be. Also that you will be treated by others exactly as you expect to be or as you indicate that you want to be.

I'm always wary of going overboard with these types of strategies, but I do believe that there is quite some truth in the thought that if you present yourself as a doormat you will be walked on. The reverse end of this spectrum of presenting yourself as a king or queen and then expecting to be worshipped does not necessarily follow.

I think there is more to be said for ensuring that you present yourself as a person who is aware of your own worth as a human being and thereby setting a base line to ensure that you have a platform from which to build personal success.

Certainly, you can work to build an image of yourself as an achiever, but it will normally take a lot more than just rhetoric about how wonderful you are.

Making sure you present yourself as someone who won't be trodden on is definitely a strategy to go with. I would be a little more wary about the prospects of following on with image building based on dreams alone. This is really an area where achievement by action rather than words is the order of the day.

Approach each day with a fresh outlook

One of the very positive things that successful people are able to do is approach each new day with a fresh outlook. They leave their dirty laundry from yesterday behind them if they had a bad day and don't harbor the thought that it's the beginning of an unhealthy trend.

I don't think there would be anybody who hasn't had at least one bad day and we have probably all had more than our fair share at different times. The trick to personal success lies in realizing that most days are very positive and you can have an impact on just how many of are positive by maintaining your own belief that a fresh approach to each day puts the odds in your favor.

The key to this positive mental outlook on each day of course is to realize that outlook means a forward, not a rear guard analysis. Concentrating on what <u>will</u> be and not what <u>has been</u> is merely habit and can be very profitably combined with a strategy of guiding the day rather than letting it guide you.

I am not suggesting that you forget the importance of preparation, strategy, and so on and that you just leave your fate to the wind, but you should add to your planning and implementation actions, the strong sense that a new day means new opportunities.

So as each day comes, look forward, think positive and leave any negative experiences in the past where they belong.

Happiness in Happiness out (HiHo)

So what is a quick way of getting positive brain food into your system to help you feel better and be more productive? The computer industry has used a very effective acronym called GiGo (Garbage in Garbage out) to capture the danger of assuming that a computer can automatically make sense out of nonsense. Although the human brain is intellectually capable of producing sense from nonsense, emotionally it has much more difficulty.

The human brain copes much better, as does the computer interestingly enough, in a summarizing role rather than in a complete translation role. In other words you'll always have some residual from the raw input to the human brain with what comes out the other side.

For this reason, Hi Ho (happiness in, happiness out) makes a lot of sense. The more happy statements, visions, musical sounds and feelings you can get going into the body the more happy feelings will be in there and the more likely it is that happiness will be the resultant effect in terms of output.

The beauty of all this is that you don't have to take my word for it. Just try playing some music that you regard as very depressing and repeat to yourself some particularly negative thing about yourself and see whether you feel super happy. Don't do this for too long by the way because it's rather unnerving and has an immediate effect.

Next, making sure you have it right on hand so you can counteract the negativity straight away, pull out some really happy music and repeat already prepared happy positive comments to yourself so that you can experience the total contrast.

So, what about all this in everyday situations? Well that's the whole point. Because you are not thinking about it all the time, you are actually letting your own HiHo (Happiness in Happiness out) turn into a GiGo (Garbage in Garbage out) and all this garbage is not automatically translated into happy thoughts.

Emotionally, the garbage you let in churns around in your mind and gives you a roller coaster ride of negativity that leaves you wondering why you are only happy for short periods of time and why that happiness is unpredictable.

Isn't it amazing how easy it is to understand your unpredictable emotions when you start thinking about the fact that, for the most part, the garbage going in is uncontrolled, unpredictable and unwelcome.

The next section on Mental Marking gives you are plan for dealing with this situation.

Mental marking

One of things I try to do in defining things that are good for me and not good for me in the brain food department is to form a mental picture of each thing that comes my way that I see as positive and surround it with stars.

If I see it as negative I put a big cross through it mentally or use one of those modern symbols with a circle and a stroke through it to indicate that it's not allowed on this patch of brain. I call this 'mental marking'.

It may sound all very humorous and even more than a little silly and melodramatic, but I find that keeping things out of your mind needs a few little tricks to prevent you falling into the traps. It's amazing how, just on a day to day basis, things that you don't really want in your head will be disguised as things that you might want and you open up your brain.

Mental marking is very easy really because all you have to do is form a suitable single image such as a book, a person, a name and then just very firmly mentally put a large black cross through it or circle it and put a stroke through if it isn't something that you want.

Hopefully by having well defined happy message seeking devices operating you'll have many more situations where you put up the same images and put a big tick next to them or surround them with stars to indicate how welcome they are into your thoughts.

And don't just use this for external thoughts. It's also very useful for things that crop up in your own thinking. Don't forget an uncontrolled brain is a random firing brain and can put up all sorts of things, some of which will be randomly negative. So if you have this technique on hand, whether it comes from within you, or without you, you'll have your system organized for labeling, sorting and culling thoughts according to whether they are positive or negative.

Finally, just because you have got a system in place to shape your thinking do not think you can relax, negativity is everywhere
.

Monitor Your State of Mind

One particular problem we all have to be aware of is the possibility that negative things around us will creep up on us and before we know it eat away at our positive attitudes and positive style.

Rationalization of substandard performance by comparing one's self constantly to those who accept lower levels of behavior is something we must all guard against.

A handy little technique for making sure that your standards don't slip is keeping a diary of personal achievements as represented by long standing permanent changes in your personal situation or day to day behavior that you have worked towards and achieved.

Referring to this diarized list of achievements on a monthly basis helps you keep yourself on track in terms of never giving up any ground that you have gained even if you may not, at the time, be succeeding in your quest to break new ground.

As is said in so many situations, it's not possible to do anything about change unless you know that change is happening. The same thing applies to monitoring the lifelong quest for personal success.

So keep your record of achievements as proudly as if they were in the Guinness Book of Records. They are more important to your personal success than world records. Set your standard and move up from there.

In addition, this review system has the added benefit that you have a written record of your strengths and how they are growing as you eliminate little weaknesses.

Use the media

Many people say that the expansion of the media, particularly on the World Wide Web has contributed significantly to people losing control of the happiness component of their lives. I don't agree with this because I believe that the human mind has the most amazing capacity to control inputs if it has a 'mind' to do so.

The habits that we have in accepting what other people tell us, just far too readily, have been well developed for hundreds and probably thousands of years if we are to believe the details available in relation to behavior of human beings thousands of years ago.

Modern media, however, can provide an opportunity for you to select many happy inputs that can make your internal state and use of external output just that much more positive and powerful.

Obviously, the capacity for garbage in remains the same, but that will never change. This is why the onus for creating the internal state to manage the garbage that exists externally is always going to remain with you and the skill you develop to do that is going to be useful to you for as long as you live.

This issue of how you live and why you choose the path you follow, whether you have one, two or two hundred lives, still comes back to how you live from a day to day point of view and taking responsibility for the positives and the negatives.

The way I see it, if you do have two hundred lives then you have a spirit that you need to be working on right now because feeding that spirit happiness is going to be a habit that will be of benefit to you on such a longer term basis. If on the other hand you only have one life, the same principle applies because you need to be getting as much out of this life as you possibly can by feeding that spirit as much happiness as you can possibly find.

To me the important argument in this whole exercise is the fact that it recognizes that human beings are spiritual beings that need to feed that spirit in a positive way.

Without a positive spirit, there is no hope. Without hope, there is no spirit at all.

Another powerful argument for getting into spiritual feeding is that it's absolutely free. You can have a virtual, spiritual feeding frenzy and it doesn't cost you anything. And quite the opposite of having a physical feeding frenzy, there are no negative after affects. Quite the contrary the positive after effects are amazingly long lasting. Also, unlike physical feeding, you don't have to restrict yourself to three meals a day you can just be eating spiritual food all the time.

Once you have converted to a positive spirit diet, you can start to share the recipe with friends and family, but be prepared for some skepticism as things that are free and good for you are usually looked at with suspicion. Maybe you will need to wait to be asked and let the message come out naturally.

Play the right music

Music is a very individual thing as is the human voice and the human fingerprint. Music is also present in our daily lives on an escapable basis. One thing we all know is that certain songs and tunes make us feel particularly good, we sing along, we remember, we associate them with good things.

What many of us fail to recognize is that negative emotions can also be raised or associated with music. This makes this special happiness in component, which is so strong in music, one that needs to be controlled.

Many people would say that they could define everyone's happiness in a musical formula. If this were so, there would not be the thousands of failures in the music industry for every single hit that comes along. And the predictability of what did constitute a hit would not be such a haphazard activity.

Fortunately, one of the big benefits of modern technology is the capacity to totally control your auditory environment in almost every circumstance.

An added bonus is that controlling this auditory environment has a double whammy effect because the actual involvement in the programming of your own auditory input can be so intrinsically rewarding and give you a still greater high because of that feeling of control over your inputs and outputs.

All that is required is a true and sensitive assessment of your feelings in relation to the wide variety of auditory inputs that are available to you each day.

With a little extra sensitivity it will not be hard for you to identify how any feelings of negativity are associated with certain music or sounds and how your positive feelings are associated with other music and sounds.

Then, with the amount of control that you can bring into this area you can start to increase amazingly quickly the positives at the expense of the negatives.

Unfortunately, it's not as easy as just selecting certain performers or composers because performers and composers are people and they have mood swings as much as we do. Sometimes their most brilliant works from a technical point of view are the most negative emotionally.

Some people say that to cross out the black components will make you artistically and emotionally stunted. While I understand the argument and can appreciate the motives behind it, it is not one that I support. I stand by the formula of happiness in, happiness out and that part happiness in equals part happiness out.[5]

---

[5] The argument that there cannot be good without evil and so on is a complex one and central to Zen Buddhism, so if you did not pursue my previous reference to Zen, this is yet another opportunity to see how it takes the concept of the role of the mind in personal contentment to a whole other level.

Select Your Acquaintances

Snobbery is such a negative word for most people, but strangely it has a message for all of us if only we would change the word to selectivity. Selectivity is all about selecting the people you choose to associate with to ensure that you only get positive messages sent towards you.

This is not egotism in the sense of the positive messages being positive messages about yourself, but wholly geared towards maintaining a positive outlook by making sure that the things around you have a positive vibration. As I've said so many times, it's amazing how examples from nature can help us understand these phenomena.

For example, if you have a barrel full of apples and throw in one rotten apple before very long the whole barrel of apples would be rotten.

If you have one rotten apple in the bottom of a barrel and fill the barrel with good apples after a very short time, the barrel will still be full of rotten apples. To me this is nature's way of showing us that a small amount of negativity grows very quickly and is virtually unstoppable.

So if you want to avoid going rotten you have to keep company with good apples and develop the skills to recognize the rotten apples by the vibrations they give off.

The best way to recognize these vibrations is that they will leave you feeling negative, drained and doubting yourself.

Good influences come from people who vibrate positive energy that makes you feel confident.

Just use your feelings to pick the good from the bad, it's not that hard.

Positive mental attitude

In terms of personal success many people just speak in a hyperactive way about always maintaining a positive mental attitude as though this will solve all problems.

In my view, having a positive mental attitude is very important but only as a facilitative component used in conjunction with carefully planned and implemented strategies.

The reason positive mental attitude gets so much attention is because its characteristic as a lubricating fluid on the machinery for achieving success is so critical.

For this reason, I often tell people to think about positive mental attitude in exactly this way. If you don't lubricate machinery it very quickly starts to run poorly and then breaks down or seizes up and has to be thrown away.

You should think of your Personal Success Strategies in the same context. Your strategies and skill are the machinery and the positive mental attitude is the lubricant.

Thinking about positive mental attitude in this way makes it much more meaningful because it takes away the vagueness of where being positive fits into the whole picture of success.

The key aspect of this analogy is the way it reinforces the need for an ongoing positive approach. In addition, it lets you move past the rah-rah aspect of positive thinking and accept it as a useful adjunct in approaching your challenges.

You'll find positive thinking more useful if you see it as part of an overall approach to life and achieving personal success that combines with skill and hard work.

Be convinced

If you are still skeptical about the role of a positive mental attitude, it is because one of the essential elements of introducing a positive approach to life is to be convinced that it will actually work. Some people actually approach the actual process of being positive with a negative attitude. It's no wonder that there is no result.

It is essential that you remain totally convinced that being positive in every way is part of getting you a positive result.

I use the happiness in - happiness out philosophy because it gives such a good understanding that if you don't feed in anything negative, nothing negative can come out the other side unless you introduce it yourself. Furthermore, if your super busy introducing positives and blocking the entry of any negatives, you will be so busy you won't have time to introduce any negatives.

In the final analysis, you've got to be convinced that being positive and working on a happiness in - happiness out philosophy will work. Similarly, you've got to be convincing in talking to other people about it, in fact, being convincing in talking to other people about it, is one of the key blocking strategies to prevent negativity coming into your system.

So there it is. Happiness in equals happiness out. All you have to do is turn your back on the garbage in, garbage out philosophy which pervades most people's lives. This really isn't that hard to do if you suddenly realize that a lot of what comes your way and that you accept without any scrutiny, is garbage. So say no to garbage, say yes to happiness in, and happiness out and it will work for you.

Having looked inward, it is time to look outward and consider the role of interpersonal interactions on our quest for personal success.

Getting on with people

All of us have situations where we meet people that we just do not like. Sometimes, however, these people are part of our circle of acquaintances or family and we have to make an effort to be friendly. How can this be achieved?

One technique I have suggested on many occasions is to take the challenge head on and do the one thing that you least feel like doing, particularly when this involves speaking to people.

If your natural tendency is to avoid someone in your family or circle of acquaintances, I recommend that you set the challenge of approaching and speaking to this person.

What you will find is that once you get close to the person your mental barriers about them will start to break down. But keep in mind, this technique is designed for dealing with people for whom you have an unnatural dislike.

If you have a very good reason for disliking them, especially if they do not like you and are very likely to be rude, then do not use this technique because you are probably avoiding them for a very good reason.

Only use this technique where there is absolutely no logical reason why you should not get on with the person involved. I think you will find it very helpful.

Avoid the meanies

It is always sad to meet someone who confirms that there are people out there who are just outright mean. Unfortunately, it is a fact of life that the normal curve is alive and well and there are just as many really bad people as there are really nice people. Furthermore, when one of these people gets into a position where they can influence the lives of many others, there is not normally a lot that can be done about it by the people under most threat.

This is one of those few occasions where I have to support the strategy of beating a hasty retreat. If you can't change the situation, suffering is definitely not a recipe for success. You are far better advised to move on and find another situation where the people that you work with, or for, are human beings who create an atmosphere of pleasure, achievement and overall success in a team environment.

So if you get caught in this type of situation don't hesitate to make the move elsewhere. Don't feel that you have to be a martyr and suffer. Put all your energy into finding a suitable alternative.

Remember personal success is not about winning battles, it's about enjoying the challenges of life.

Life is a journey not a destination and the company you keep is a key part of that journey.

In fact, part of personal success planning is making sure you never end up working with or for the 'meanies' of the world. Learn to identify these 'meanies' and you will be able to avoid them and make your path to personal success that much more enjoyable, and shorter. Having the opportunity to make a choice is the first part of this process, exercising the choice opportunity is the second.

Be friendly

As I was coming off the golf course recently I was giving the great Australian salute by waving some flies away from my face. Suddenly, I noticed two people in a car waving happily to me as they drove out of the golf club.

Just as a natural reaction I waved back at them thinking they were waving at me. Only moments later did I realize that they were waving at me because they had interpreted my great Australian salute as a cheery greeting.

This incident made me think how important it is to be naturally open and friendly. The success that comes from just a friendly open style is not usually associated with the achievement of any external goal, but it can contribute so much to the achievement of your personal goals in interactions with other human beings.

The tradition of waving to someone you see on a country road is something that has sadly disappeared long ago amongst city people. Nevertheless, the feeling of belonging that this symbolizes has not disappeared and it is something that can be experienced by all of us, particularly if we are a little more friendly and liberal with our greetings.

Just a little more friendliness can make you much more personally contented and you may be pleasantly surprised at some of the outcomes in terms of other people's behavior.

Celebrate the success of others

It still amazes me how many people don't enjoy seeing the success of others. You should not ever consider that another person's success means that you have failed.

Comparisons are odious and never more so than in assessing your self-worth.

Those who are working towards personal success in a constructive way will see the success of others as an opportunity to observe strategies, outcomes and rewards that they also wish to enjoy.

Feelings of jealousy, envy and so on only interfere with the constructive process of seeing the world as an essentially non-competitive self-paced opportunity to develop and succeed.

So if you have negative feelings about the success of others, switch your attention to the work they have done to succeed. You may be tempted to think that no work has been involved, but upon close examination you will see this is not the case.

Look at the effort, think about your approach, learn from others who have been there before you and aim to do as well if not better.

Control your emotions

One of the best parts of being able to feed yourself a decent quota of happy thoughts, music and so on is that you can actually decide that things that might make other people very angry, merely leave you amused or bemused.

I recall very early on when I played the occasional game of golf, without knowing anything at all about the game, being very bewildered to see people stamp their feet and throw their clubs. In one case I saw a person hit their golf cart so hard with their club that they broke the wheel of the cart and the head of the club and had to return to the clubhouse and rent a new cart for the remainder of the game.

When I later started to play more often, on a number of occasions people commented to me that they were amazed that I could play such bad shots and laugh at myself.

It's just that I find the idea of practicing regularly and playing a game where there is only one basic bodily movement that most people find very difficult quite amusing.

I mean how to make this one movement perfectly seems to escape people who work on it for ten, fifteen and fifty years. On one occasion a perfect shot can be hit and literally minutes later it is followed by a disastrous shot. I find this concept quite hilarious.

When you add to this my personal general lack of sporting skill, I operate on the principle that to remain motivated and keep playing as regularly as I do, and trying as hard as I do, I <u>need</u> to find this funny.

Creating negative thoughts by negative actions, and negative words, is going to leave me very unhappy indeed and that's not why I am playing the game.

For me feelings of bewilderment and wonder can be particularly happy ones. These are the thoughts that I create in my mind when playing golf. I am bewildered at why I cannot apply effectively the guidelines that the golfing professional has outlined for me and I wonder what the best strategy will be to improve my game and make it still more enjoyable.

On a lighter note, I often compare golf to life, no-one will ever get a hole in one on every hole on any course and get a score of 18 on a 18 hole golf course so you just have to enjoy the game, appreciate the beautiful surroundings, enjoy the feeling of swinging the club and look to make every shot you play the best one you possible can at the time by having complete control of your state of mind.

Maybe the similarities to life is why so many people persist with the game.

Count Your Blessings

I was driving along the road the other day when I saw a group of carers wheeling a number of disabled children on an outing.

This really brought home to me once more the wisdom of counting your blessings in achieving personal success in life.

My father use to repeat often one of his favorite sayings about the philosopher who said, "I thought I was badly off because I had no shoes until I saw a man with no feet".

Life is a continuum and there will always be people who are better off than you are and people who are worse off than you are. The clue to being personally successful is positioning yourself with a positive frame of mind in relation to your lot in life.

This does not mean that you base your own happiness on the unhappiness of others, but it does mean that life at all levels provides all of us with opportunities to be successful each in our own way. Making that philosophy work is all about counting your blessings in the hand that has been dealt to you in life's great card game and playing that hand in the most positive and capable way that you can.

To see these people working together to do just that made me all that more aware that mental attitude is a big percentage of personal success, and being positive takes less effort and uses less energy than being negative.[6]

Don't let others get you down

One of the areas I have worked hardest on in career development is helping people to reach their optimum level of chosen performance. Often this has involved developing strategies for dealing with spoiling tactics from' put down' people that should really be helping them.

Somehow these spoilers feel that keeping others subservient is important for maintaining their own position of strength and authority and this can make life very difficult for those who work for them or are in their social group.

---

[6] To experience an outstanding example of someone making the most of their lot in life go to the internet and marvel at the positive approach of Margaret McKerrow Schroder (1947-2013). Her autobiography is called *On the Move.*.

Unfortunately, my long term finding is that these put down people just don't change. They keep putting down people that they have some power over; usually to battle their own insecurity. For this reason, the only solution is to get out from under quickly, to a situation where you're able to control your own destiny.

If you do have to work for someone else, choose someone who will support you and open the way for you to succeed, on a basis of mutual respect and mutual achievement.

One of the worst things about these situations is that it is so difficult to see beyond life being victimized by these people when you're stuck under the influence of someone who is so negative.

Years of protecting themselves in this way has made these people particularly skilful at eroding people's confidence, and making them think that there is no way out.

Of course this is total rubbish and very often the people who are being belittled are doing very successful things in other areas, such as sport or hobbies and will be just as successful in a new supportive job environment as they are with these extra-curricular activities.

There are a few simple tests that you can use about your relationships with people in senior positions. Just ask these questions, 'Are you praised or abused?' 'Are you kept informed or kept in the dark?' and finally, 'Do you speak positively or negatively about the person you work for?' and the big one 'Do you look forward to going to work each day?'.

If you answered negatively to any of these questions you need to think very seriously about getting out and finding yourself a better life. There are good people out there, but the onus is on you to go out and find them in order to achieve personal success.

It will be tough, but you only have one life and you deserve to enjoy it.

Feed yourself positive thoughts

Following up on the concept deflecting and overcoming put downs, it is worth reflecting again on how you can control you own inputs.

It is fascinating to see that while so much attention is paid to the improvement of diet in the modern world, that there is little comparable work done on feeding yourself positive thoughts.

It seems to me that if you are what you eat in body terms then in mental terms you have to be what you see, hear, smell and touch.

With your sense of hearing accounting for the bulk of your sensory input, it would seem to make a lot of sense to control, as much as possible, the positivity of what you hear.

To do this is really quite simple because you spend all of your time in your own company and probably spend more time talking to yourself than anyone else. In other words you have almost total control over your own thoughts and the associated input unless you choose to abandon control to other forces.

No matter how it is presented, this self-talk concept makes sense. In fact it is a very deep philosophical concept that has been pondered through the ages. The trick, however, is to keep it simple and just use positive self-talk on the basis that the more positive thoughts you squeeze in the more positive you will feel and the more positive output you will achieve.

SUMMARY

Having considered some general principles and examples, these themes will help you draft your Personal Action List for this chapter:

POSITIVE BEHAVIOR

- **Accept that being positive is a choice.**
- **Use positive key words and actions to set your own emotional level.**
- **Think positive <u>then</u> consider the facts to beat negative feelings.**
- **Control your feelings by keeping <u>your</u> perspective not that of others.**

PERSONAL ACTION LIST
(Key words, actions & events to memorize, visualize and discuss)

Positive behaviors I want to develop

_____

_____

_____

_____

_____

_____

_____

_____

_____

_____

_____

_____

CHAPTER 6

Intense Behavior

For some time I have been unsure of continuing with the word intense to describe the need for passion in your life, but no other word seems to combine that need for involvement, commitment and focus.

The issue for some people is that the word intense is related to the words tense and tension, which they see as negative. But focus is not enough you have to be committed and passionate.

Having thought about it a lot, I see that the intensity component of Personal Success Strategies has a stress aspect, but I regard this as being the 'good' stress needed to meet a major challenge.

There is good stress that you get when you are gearing up to do something challenging that you really want to do and bad stress when you feel trapped and not able to handle a situation.

Intense behavior is like good stress that drives you to succeed at what you want.

So What Is Intense Behavior About?

Intense behavior means you are driven by positive thoughts and your willingness to meet the challenge brings issues closer, removes ignorance, reduces fear and increases your capacity to act.

Vague behavior, on the other hand is driven by negative thoughts and the resulting fear leaves issues at a distance, maintains ignorance, increases fear and reduces the capacity to act.

As an example, think of the situation where you have to do a test or a work assignment and how you always put off getting started until the last minute.

What happens is classic. You finally get started and then discover that you have not left yourself enough time. You do the best you can in the time available, but it is inevitably never as good as it would have been if you had been more intense (think of a combination passion, focus, commitment, enthusiasm) in your approach and had started immediately.

Definition: A developed characteristic which involves a strong degree of enthusiasm and passion, and a high level of commitment and involvement.

Example Statement: Isn't life great.

Example Actions:

- Select someone you want to be close to you and tell them your innermost feelings on a key issue.
- Pick someone who is negative and   challenge them and/or lift their spirits by saying "Isn't life great".
- List all the things in your life about which you feel really passionate.
- List your strongest character traits.

The following examples show a variety of ways that intensity opens the door to achieving what you want.

Take a Risk

So often we hear people speaking about finding a balance and harmony in their day to day activities. Certainly, this is very good advice and one of the general principles of being successful.

However, very few people who have been successful have done so without taking some personal risks. Nothing stupid, but definitely putting themselves out of their comfort zone.

It's important of course to emphasize that the advice here is towards a calculated risk. That is, prepare well for that financial commitment such as a rental property or share investment, but be prepared to get just a little bit nervous about some of the new things that you're doing.

Once again the risk need not necessarily be a financial one. It may be that you'll take some personal risks, try some new activities that you are not particularly good at, but have always wanted to do. It might be introducing yourself to that person that you've had the opportunity to speak to for some time, but didn't because you thought they would not be friendly towards you.

Whatever the challenge, throw a little bit of zest into your life and take some risks. Chances are your path to personal success will be more interesting and more fruitful.

Actions speak louder than words

In preparing a mental training program for a football team, it occurred to me again how visible actions are so much easier to judge than the vagueness of behavior.

This program involved mental training to improve physical performance on the field. If someone just can't tackle for whatever reason or can't pick the gaps to run into there is no pretending that the mental training program has worked if the person doesn't improve.

This can be a very embarrassing test of one's ability as a trainer but can also provide tremendous rewards because visible successes are just that much more dramatic than behavioral changes, which are very much judged by the eye of the beholder.

Part of being successful is realizing that demonstrable achievement is a key factor in any success story. Everyone should be looking for success that cannot be disputed. It is probably for this reason that the accumulation of wealth is so much in people's eye and that sporting achievement is so much associated with our society's heroes.

So in striving for personal success there is certainly quite some merit in finding an area where the achievements are black and white. Shades of grey are probably correctly perceived by many as the refuge of would be's and could be's rather than the genuinely successful.

Act now

One of the characteristics of people who are successful is that they act immediately when a situation demands it.

Words like procrastination and prevarication are well known in popular English language usage for a very good reason.

Many people delay and think and ponder and by the time action comes about it is far too late. It is not that people who have a successful style act without thinking, on the contrary they clarify the circumstances surrounding the situation, choose a course of action and <u>then</u> act quickly and decisively.

The aim is to strike the perfect balance between the two sayings 'They who hesitate are lost' and 'Look before you leap'. The truly successful person just seems to develop a better feel for where to go and how to get there.

Developing this decisive style is not done by some magical process. It comes about through not closing down your systems when problems arise, but remaining alert and attacking them vigorously.

So don't look upon your next problem as a reason to run away, attack it head on and you will find the solution will come to you much more quickly. As always, you will find the secret of success is constant practice. You will have to invest a fair amount of time, but the pay-off will be worth the effort.

Be competitive

There is a lot of talk these days about everybody working in a team situation and sharing the glory, the responsibility and the authority.

This is all well and good, but if you are very individually competitive, don't be put off.

Individual competitive drive and strong personal motivation have been the reason for many major outstanding achievements over the centuries. What is needed in this circumstance is that the individual is in the situation where these characteristics are needed and appreciated.

A team player in a highly individual competitive environment may not do well and neither may a highly individually competitive person do well in a team environment. So, identify your particular style and then find the environment where that style is most successful.

Matching yourself to the circumstances in sport, work or just day to day life activities is a real skill. The saying about square pegs not going into round holes illustrates how it is the match between you and the environment that is important, not just your profile.

Get the best fit for your skills and attitude and you will do very well.

Be known as an action person
How often do we hear someone say that a person has initiative or self-motivation?

By making yourself known as someone with initiative or as an action person, you will set yourself on a very quick path to success in your chosen field.

It still astounds me that there are so many people who just do not have the attitude or capacity to get on with things.

Many years ago an acquaintance of mine stepped through a glass door in a terrible horrific accident. Everyone who was present just stood and stared as glass shattered all around him and cut him deeply on the arms, back and legs. He was the most composed of all and had to yell 'get organized' and a very brief description of what he thought of the group who were watching him about to bleed to death.

He was well known as an action man and success came to him in all areas for that reason. This small, but very significant, example of how he acted in an emergency is a good illustration of the type of attitude that brings personal success.

I certainly don't suggest putting yourself in dangerous situations to test your capacity but do think about how quickly you react on projects that you decide to undertake or how ready you are to present new ideas and help other people. You may find that you don't really rate as well as you would like and need to give yourself a hurry-along, talking to or kick up the back-side to succeed.

Be personally resourceful and innovative

It is a fallacy that being innovative or personally resourceful is the province of a very small percentage of the population.

All of us have the capacity to be inventive in so many ways. Once we get it clear in our minds that we can think of better ways of doing things we open up a whole realm of new experiences.

It really is as simple as believing that you can and will think of better ways of doing things. One of the major drawbacks of most educational systems is that they educate people not only just using the information provided in the curriculum, but with the added thought that there is nothing more. In other words, everything that is worth knowing has been thought of and being inventive isn't part of the equation.

If you've now reached your 30th, 40th, 50th year or your 90th year for that matter and haven't got that innovative philosophy, don't despair, it really is just a matter of changing your whole way of thinking, and starting slowly is no problem.

Depending upon your personality, you may want to work independently, by changing some basic home routines. Alternatively, you may decide to study up using any of the numerous books published by authors in the areas of creativity and innovation.

Whatever technique you use, it will almost certainly bring instant results. The real skill is in persisting with your efforts and turning those initial inspiring experiences into longer term changes in your style to make you more practically resourceful and innovative in the long term.

Careful use of resources

There has been a lot of talk in business particularly about efficiency and effectiveness for a very long time.

This is for a good reason, because these two characteristics of efficiency and effectiveness are very important for day to day activities in all our lives.

Efficiency is all about making the best possible use of our resources without waste. Effectiveness is about applying our resources to get the best possible outcome with the tools we have available.

This situation is very beautifully illustrated by the expression of the 24 egg omelet. This is usually used to describe the person who can make a beautiful looking and delicious omelet, but uses two dozen eggs in the process. They are highly effective in making a beautiful omelet but terribly inefficient in the use of resources.

At the other end of the scale is the person who makes omelets that will feed twice as many people, but waters down the eggs to achieve the result. This is a great use of resources but not very effective.

The person who is both efficient and effective uses milk to make the omelet in just the right proportion to make a delicious omelet but making the eggs go the maximum possible distance.

All of us are faced with the challenge of efficiency and effectiveness every day. The person who will be highly successful is the one who is able to balance the quality of the final product with the need to make maximum use of the resources.

Concentrate and focus

Some time ago I had the pleasure of conducting a number of personal success training sessions for a group of young sports people.

It was interesting to see how much Personal Success Strategies training did apply to the circumstances of these young people looking to make a career in their chosen sport. Similarly, it seems their various characteristics of commitment, concentration and mental focus certainly had a lot to contribute to success in life.

In talking about concentration and focus, I highlighted several areas for special attention in the personal success area:
1)   Setting goals and working towards their achievement.
2)   An obsession about their particular goals
3)   A sense of urgency has very often been associated with success and I see it as essential as it contributes significantly to concentration and focus in the achievement of short-term goals.

4)   Accepting responsibility for your own actions plus an overall sense of social responsibility.

5)   Total concentration and focus.

Anyone can use techniques for personal concentration and focus to achieve goals. As I indicated to this group, it is important to realize that, as with any other skills, these skills must be practiced and perfected before there can be any expectation of a positive benefit.

Consider alternatives

There is an old saying that when one door closes another door opens. However, you really have to be very positive about alternatives if something you have been pursuing is suddenly out of your reach.

It's very important if you've been pursuing a goal or had your heart set on some particular thing that will just never happen, that you do not allow this to cloud your whole horizon so that you do not consider other opportunities which may in the final analysis be just as good or better.

I have spoken over the years to many people whose opportunity to do a course of study for example never eventuated, but by bouncing back and considering other options these people ended up having a very successful career. Others on the contrary saw the initial setback as being almost a final statement that they would never achieve life's' goals and dropped their bundle, so to speak, and did not put the same amount of energy into pursuing good alternatives.

Life is just an endless series of pathways and it is a mistake to ever feel that it is just a highway where a roadblock means that you have literally reached the end of the road.

So if you want to be successful, just consider how many options there are and realize that just because you happen to focus on one thing for the time being doesn't mean you have to forget all the others that are available to you if you need them.

Define those top qualities

One thing we should all do in our quest for personal success is make sure that we are very clear about what the required attributes for making our life a success are most likely to be.

Doing a mini audit on your skills and comparing your skills to the challenges that you are undertaking let you get a much clearer picture of the strategies that you should implement to capitalize on your opportunities.

In business, a SWOT analysis means looking at strengths, weaknesses, opportunities and threats, S-W-O-T. This is just as important in personal success.

It's a very simple process, you just list your strengths, your weaknesses, what opportunities are available to you in the world at large and what are the threats to you achieving overall personal success.

You can then list your objectives, where you want to go, and your strategies, how you plan to get there, in full awareness of the tools you have available to you.

This mini audit should be a regular part of your personal planning as it should be part of all business planning.

The best part is that this should not be a chore. It's a really enjoyable exercise that you will find fulfilling in the short, medium and long term.

Also, by keeping your SWOT analysis sheets you can see where you've come from and often get a clearer picture of the way ahead.

So get in the habit of listing those strengths, weaknesses, opportunities and threats, and objectives and strategies for success will follow.

Developing good habits

I spoke recently to a person who was concerned that developing good habits meant losing control of your life and living like a robot.

This is certainly not the case. If you have worked out a situation where being in a routine helps you achieve goals that you have decided are important to you then habits are terrific tools for being successful.

In fact, in changing behaviors you are not happy with, developing a routine that substitutes a new behavior for the old behavior is highly desirable. If you find you can't control your weight for example because every night you sit down in front of the TV with a big helping of some desert followed by chocolates, then developing a routine where you serve, wrap up and freeze seven small desserts for the week, preferably after you have just eaten a huge dessert and don't feel particularly hungry, can be very productive.

Habits do not have to be bad habits and, like the case of the champion sportsman who could never remember a single day when he did not exercise, they can be good habits even when they are obsessive and completely bound up with your whole way of life. So, just sort out the habits that work for you and build them into your routine. They are part of you successfully managing your life.

Developing good study habits

Invariably when you speak to people about study and success, they have a lot of problems, particularly with procrastination.

One of the small techniques that I have found particularly helpful in overcoming that study procrastination problem is launching into the project as early as possible.

One of the reasons that people have severe problems with study and procrastinate is their fear that they will not be able to cope with the challenge. When you launch yourself into it immediately, you get close to the problem and discover that it is not as daunting as you thought.

If you avoid the study situation your fear level is maintained and eventually when you are forced to get into the situation you discover it is not so daunting but you have inevitably left yourself too little time to use your new found knowledge about your ability to cope.

So if you want to beat that study habit problem, launch into the work at the earliest possible time, you won't find it anywhere near as difficult as you imagined it to be and you will have the time to do a really good job.

Intrinsic reward

One of the most powerful ways of developing new behaviors is to set up an intrinsic reward loop. Basically, the best way to develop a permanent new behavior is for it to be rewarding in its own right and not on the basis of some future reward that it will bring.

If you are looking to achieve some major goal, a very good strategy is to identify one part of the path towards that goal that you will find immediately rewarding. If you can establish that behavior strongly in your overall life activities you can start to bring other aspects of the overall goal into the loop.

For example if your major goal is to get up every morning and walk for five kilometers, come back, have a leisurely breakfast and read the morning paper, but you find the thought of getting up early and exercising totally abhorrent, you need to find the element of that total behavior that will be most internally (intrinsically) rewarding.

It will most likely be having a leisurely breakfast and reading the paper. So, to work your way towards the bigger goal you should start by only getting up earlier and having the leisurely breakfast and reading the paper. Do no more in the way of heading towards your exercise goal until you have established the breakfast and newspaper routine so strongly that if you don't do it, things just don't seem right.

You can then stretch yourself to the very small extent of getting dressed and going outside or to the area where you exercise (if you are inside), and just sitting quietly and relaxing or just taking some deep breaths, but still restricting yourself to activities that are immediately rewarding.

As you work each phase of the intrinsically rewarding activities into your routine it becomes that much easier to move to the next phase. Fascinatingly, if you break for some reason from the routine to travel or whatever, it is amazing how the various reward patterns are retained separately and allow you to redevelop the total program that much more quickly.

Once again, the whole principle is centered on controlling your feedback to yourself.

By retaining total control over the reward process you get a double benefit because the feeling of reward is that much greater when it is controlled by you and your ability to withstand the influence of outside events is that much greater because you have more control.

Develop people skills

I spoke recently with an executive who I knew to be highly intelligent and skilful and in many ways this person had been very successful. However, he found that his further development was blocked by his inability to work well with people in difficult situations.

Interpersonal or people skills are vital for success in every situation. Even if they are not the central theme of your activities, such as with highly technical positions that require little interaction, they still are required professionally and socially.

Like any skill, if you just step out and try some particular social technique live for the first time it will not normally go well. Practice makes perfect with interpersonal skills as it does with any sporting activity and you have to be prepared to invest the time in thinking and strategizing about what you are going to say and rehearsing the lines in your mind.

So if you have problems in this particularly important area, put together a suitable formal or informal training course, and then practice, practice, practice.

You will find that even the most basic improvement in how you deal with people on a day to day basis will make you feel much happier. One success will lead to another in your quest for better interpersonal skills.

Rehearse Your Lines

So often hints about self-confidence are just so vague and don't really tell you anything other than you should be self-confident and it will be much better for you.

One of the things that I often tell people is the great benefit of mentally rehearsing what you would say in a difficult situation that you know is coming up.

Imagine yourself in that situation and then say to yourself, or say out loud depending upon the circumstances, exactly what you would like to say on the day.

So often we all think about difficult situations where we didn't say exactly what we would have liked. This is the classic, 'oh, if only I had thought of that' situation..

Rehearsing what you will say in a difficult situation that is coming up is how to overcome that feeling of regret of not being fully prepared.

So if you know about a situation that is coming up that may be emotionally grueling, like asking for a pay rise or negotiating something difficult at work or with a family member, live the experience in your mind and practice what you want to say.

It may not come out exactly like that on the day but you will certainly be better prepared and speak with much more self-confidence than if you just play it by ear. Just the smallest amount of preparation can pay dividends, but investing more time gives you a better chance of a good outcome on that one occasion and also starts the process of doing the same thing in the future.

Develop your own reward system

It is interesting with all the talk about macro economics and micro economics that so little attention is paid to individual economics.

We all have our little economic system revolving around our day to day activities and a better understanding of it can help us greatly in motivating us to achieve our goals.

The beauty of this individual economy is that it is controlled by you. You're the Treasurer, the Prime Minister or the President or whatever title you want to give yourself and you can choose to impose taxes, give windfall gains, or administer any plus or minus you feel like.

Too often we all look outside our own individual economy and think that all those micro economic pressures in relation to our day to day bill paying and earning and the macro economic pressures from world events have us totally at their mercy. The fact is, in pure enjoyment terms, they're pretty far removed from the personal enjoyment decisions you can make about things as basic but highly pleasurable as going to sit outside in the sun for half an hour.

So if you've got a bit of a fixation about events that are outside you, and probably beyond your control, try focusing in. It won't take you long to work out just how many things there are that you can control. The crazy thing about it is, they're all happening regularly on a day to day basis and you're letting all the fun of controlling them slip right through your fingers.

Living for today is not escapism it's an essential part of enjoying life.

Set small goals first

Over many years there have been endless conversations about motivation. How do we get motivated?

Certainly, a technique that has been used successfully by many people is setting small achievable goals and building up from there.

Proceeding in a step by step fashion has worked for many people, whether it is in starting an exercise program, giving up smoking or trying to meet any sort of personal target.

It is an interesting psychological phenomenon that to be motivating for most people goals have to be just the right distance away. If they are too far, or too close, people usually become de-motivated.

So if you're having problems getting yourself motivated have a look at the targets you are setting. They may just be too far away. Try to make them small bite size chunks and build on your successes. You will find yourself approaching that distant target much more rapidly than you expected.

Don't sell yourself short

So often we just do not give ourselves sufficient credit for the quality of our skills and the achievements that we have behind us.

It is important to realize your self-worth without becoming full of your own self-importance so that you can represent yourself properly in any situation.

Many times I have had to counsel people who have been exploited in the workplace. This exploitation often came about because of the individual's poor economic circumstances and the pressure this put on them.

Particularly when you seem under pressure and there is no one around who can help you it is important to give yourself credit for the skills that you have and to make sure that you are not exploited.

There are of course government agencies that can help you but so often the situations are marginal and it is your own self-esteem and self-confidence that is needed to win the day.

So don't underrate yourself and don't let other people underrate you.

Effort versus results

Over the years, I have had numerous opportunities to assess people accurately by virtue of the results that they achieve.

This has really confirmed in my mind the belief that appearance of activity is totally unrelated to actual results.

One employee, who I recall vividly, worked virtually the minimum prescribed hours. However, when he was at work, he did nothing but work and he worked to 100% of his capacity.

Strangely, the ability to work to 100% capacity is very rare. Needless to say, the individual that works in this way achieves the same outstanding results as my very memorable employee. The key factor in being successful is to determine very clearly what brings results and work with that formula to make the best use of your time.

It is a fact that we all fall into habit patterns, whether they are good or bad, and developing good habit patterns is just a matter of hard work, setting small and then larger goals for change, and sticking to what we resolve.

Of course, there are numerous distractions for any course of change but in this area, being successful comes back to you and the questions of motivation, resolve, and effort versus results.

Successful people take responsibility for their own lives, work out the success formula for them and apply it.

They also keep their plan up to date and adjust it to meet the changing circumstances. The key to this process is to do your planning, use your plan, check that it is effective and make it a basic part of your life.

Every dog does not have its day

There is a very popular saying that every dog has its day. It is a saying popularized by people who believe that chance and fate should play a bigger part in their success or failure than their own efforts. People do not all get their just desserts, every dog does not have its day. Some people just continue to win while others lose.

If you want to be successful then do not develop the habit of shrugging your shoulders and saying that a failure will be sorted out in the swings and roundabouts. A failure is exactly that - a failure. I am not suggesting that you need to beat yourself up every time you fail to achieve your goals. Just do not rationalize everything by saying it will work out better next time because that will be fair.

Have you ever noticed how some people seem to bob up in the headlines all the time? Some people seem to win all the time. That is not an accident. Those people put in the effort and work very hard to succeed.

So if you want to be successful; get stuck into it, make every goal post a winner. Winning and losing can both become habits and the key to success is choosing to win.

Focus

One of the key characteristics for being successful is the capacity to focus very clearly on your target.

It is almost as though you must draw mentally two big black lines down the edges of your vision to keep distractions away from your image of what you wish to achieve.

Certainly, people that are very successful not only have obsessive thoughts about their goal but they also have the ability to block out thoughts that intrude on their progress towards achieving what they want.

It is a situation very similar to meditation where you have to aim to focus on smaller and smaller images to build your mental concentration. Intense focus on goal achievement is very much the same.

The more clearly it seems that you can build a picture of that goal you are aiming for, the more likely it is that you will be able to persevere with activities that are directed towards the goal.

So if you have a goal in mind, don't be concerned if you dream about it, think about it all day and just can't get it out of your mind, this is a very positive indication that you are focused on it very clearly and will work very constructively towards its achievement.

SUMMARY

These themes will help you draft your Personal Action List for this chapter:

INTENSE BEHAVIOUR

- **Project your positive attitude.**
- **Act, don't react.**
- **Move close to remove ignorance and fear.**
- **Enjoy having and sharing emotions.**

Personal Action List
(Key words, actions & events to memorize, visualize and discuss)

Intense behaviors I want to develop

_____

_____

_____

_____

_____

_____

_____

_____

_____

_____

_____

_____

_____

_____

_____

_____

_____

_____

CHAPTER 7

Independent-minded Behavior

Independent-mindedness confirms you as the focus of decision making and makes you personally secure, able to stand firm and reject negative influences, leaving you feeling positive, powerful, satisfied and secure.

Its opposite, dependent mindedness confirms others as the focus of decision making and makes you personally insecure, unable to stand firm against negative influences which dominate you and leave you feeling negative, frustrated and wanting to escape.

Consider the classic situation where you are in a group of people and you wait for others to say what they think to make sure you do not make yourself the odd person out.

Worse still, do you say what you really think and then change it because you find yourself the odd one out. Wanting to be accepted is natural, but if you compromise yourself to gain acceptance, the price may be too great, lowering your self esteem and starting an unhealthy pattern.

Definition: To have an opinion that does not need to be tested with anybody else.

Statement: I know how I feel.

Actions:
- Write down the one thing about yourself that you like the most.
- List three people close to you who   never put you down.
- Practice assessing people on how supportive they are of others.
- Seek and weigh up advice on a key issue from an astute but supportive person.

There are so many areas where being independent-minded is the vital ingredient in being successful and I could not hope to cover them all. I have tried to include the most personal ones so that you see clearly the important link between independent-mindedness and self esteem.

Self Image

One area where you have to be constantly alert to the effects of the eroding forces around you is your image of yourself and your overall self-esteem.

I spoke to an apparently very confident woman who is pursuing a very successful career in the military. Despite her confidence at this point in her career, she recounted somewhat sadly her days at the military academy, where she and other women missed meals just to avoid the derisive comments of the male cadets.

In addition, she indicated an expectation that the same derisive comments would still be made. Why would such destructive behavior take place in an organization designed to develop confidence, leadership and teamwork?

The answer of course, is the insecurity of the males involved, and their consequent use of a heavily developed female stereotype in an attempt to promote low self esteem through failure to meet an unrealistic 'model like' body image.

This is a classic example of the need to maintain a positive self image. Too often in our society others will seek to reduce your self-image with the aim of offering you solutions that are for their own commercial game, or in the case of individuals, to boost their own confidence.

There is so much of this behavior that maintaining your self-image through positive association in the face of negative input from the community generally is a key part of personal success.

Walk tall

Many years ago there was a great Australian song with the words 'Walk tall walk straight and look the world right in the eye.[7] It amazes me how many young people tend to walk in a slouched manner with their eye directed firmly at the ground. Also, they often have a similar attitude, being downcast and pessimistic.

Can one affect the other? Well I certainly believe that approaching life in a positive manner begins not just with physical fitness but with an alert style shown by an erect posture, a confident look and generally purposeful movement.

Walking tall and thinking tall go together and a successful approach to life has as much to do with your physical approach to people as well as your mental approach. Noting that walking tall is not referring to you height, it referring to your attitude. I had to get that out there.

Interestingly, I believe the capacity to walk tall flows backwards from thinking tall. If you do not have a positive approach it is often because you lack confidence in your ability to deal with the day's challenges.

To improve in this area you have to psych yourself up and use your improved attitude to progressively knock over some slightly bigger challenges and reinforcing the positive impact of a better overall approach. You can move on from there to bigger and better things.

It's definitely not easy to do if you have been in the habit of slumping along and the road may be hard with a lot of disappointments, but persevere as improvements in this area can be very rewarding and often snowball into a whole new approach to achieving personal success.

---

[7] *Walk Tall* written by Don Young, Wallaby Music, Sydney, circa 1964.

Self sufficiency

One key characteristic of many very successful people has been their personal self sufficiency. That is, they have not felt the need to gain approval from other people for the activities that they undertake.

It is not that these people are anti-social by not liking people or by wanting to do things that are unconventional, although this sometime happens with the more eccentric. The key element is their belief in their own ideas and their lack of any need to have the approval or confirmation of others before proceeding with their strategies.

This is a very simple concept to understand but a difficult one to implement if it does not come naturally.

There have been countless books written about this characteristic with authors setting out painstakingly the negative aspect of looking for other peoples' approval and thereby emphasizing the healthy nature of being your own counselor.

So if you are already a person who is prepared to go their own way in decision making and you mostly pick the right way, do not feel that there is anything negative about this characteristic.

The only thing that you may want to do is just liaise a little more with those around you to ensure that your independent decision making and action is not seen as a reflection upon them. Let them see your independent lifestyle for what it is - a choice to be self governing.

Be an individual

Many so-called 'preachers' of success recommend particular avenues for achieving your goals.

Very often they suggest that you should follow very set guidelines and do not engage in any free thinking or erratic behavior.

In my view, it is very important to remember that you are an individual and that if we eliminated the individual behavior out of the path to success, many geniuses would never have contributed some of the greatest ideas and inventions that the world has seen.

So while setting of goals and careful planning for their achievement is a vital part of success, one should never ignore the creative component and the need for letting the spirit run free with a good idea.

All of this goes to reinforce the view that we are all individuals and should maintain our individuality no matter what system we adopt for finding success.

So look inside yourself and do not let systems take over the part of you that makes you unique. Your uniqueness is vital to your well being and success in life.

Beware the self interest of others

While I always recommend an open and friendly approach to people, it is wise to be on the lookout for that small percentage of the population who put their own interest well in advance of your own and are essentially there to rip you off.

Recently, I encountered a person who was having a run of bad luck with some injuries and was looking for some assistance to cope. He showed me an opportunity that existed to get on a mailing list for employment assistance that involved a weekly payment.

Having been a very successful individual with great confidence up to the time of his rather severe accident, this person was alert to the fact that this probably was not going to be a good investment. Because his confidence had been affected by his accident, he was wavering.

I was able to confirm his own suspicions that he could make far better use of the money than paying it to a service that was unlikely to ever be of use to him.

One particular skill in being successful is being aware of the difference between people who have a general skill to provide that will help you succeed and those who are preying on the temporary difficulties of others.

Watch out for the would be's if they could be's.

It always astounds me how people just keep cropping up who think that to be successful they must put themselves above others.

Recently, an organization that my team works with on a regular basis had reason to call seeking some information. The person that called insisted on speaking to me and would not convey any details about what they wanted done.

From my understanding of the general circumstances of the situation, much more information could have been given that would have made it much easier to arrive at a solution quickly.

Unfortunately, the person who called was much more concerned about maintaining their level of importance in their own mind by dealing directly with me rather than resolving the issue for the customer involved. This type of behavior was not only totally disrespectful of the people in my team who can do the work and only wish to get a good result, but also stands in the way of good customer service.

It's unfortunately the case that some people work on the principle that you should never let the real demands of the situation get in the way of keeping your ego intact or giving it a boost at someone else's expense.

To me, people with this sort of attitude are on the wrong track, true personal success is about getting personal ego fulfillment by working at the right level, with the right people to get the right result.

Control, don't be controlled

One of the biggest mistakes people can make in their personal organizing is allowing other people to jerk them around and make them fit in with the priorities of others at the expense of their own program.

Without being exploitive of other people, it's very important to set your focus in relation to what you want to achieve and to make sure you don't become a puppet or a bouncing ball that responds just too readily to the beck and call of other people.

A great strategy for getting under way with this focusing strategy is to use the eighty-twenty rule that says that 20% of what you do is going to account for 80% of the result you get.

At first you are going to need to think very carefully and spend what seems an inordinate amount of time deciding whether what you are about to do is part of the twenty percent that gives you 80% of the effect or part of the 80% that gives you only 20% of the effect.

Fortunately the beauty of this process is that the habit of assessing things can be learned quickly and then applied quite easily, bringing about an overall improvement in the use of your time and personal resources.

It may be something of a slow painful beginning but it's well worth it to establish a permanent focus on being in control of those factors which contribute most to your success. So get into the habit of closely scanning other people's demands and checking them against your agenda and you will find you are more likely to keep control.

Use peer group pressure correctly

The example of a full barrel of good apples not being able to make a rotten apple good again is just a tremendous example of the role of peer group pressure in our everyday lives.

Many people think that if sufficient peer group pressure is exerted that someone who is a total non-conformist will be 'cured' if they are brought into the group. My finding in general situations in the community and in business is quite the opposite. If a person is accepted into the group without any requirement to change their ways they have no incentive whatever to do so after they have been accepted.

On the contrary, if maintaining a change in whatever behavior or attitude that they have had is a pre-requisite for joining the group, then the force for change is real and seems to be much more effective. In your own day to day activities it is very wise to look at group standards and to apply these rules.

In the reverse sense peer group pressure is very important because, if you work on the principle that you are prepared to join a group that does not operate on similar standards to yourself, you may need to change your standards before you join the group. By acknowledging this, you will have a much clearer indication of what joining that group will mean for your day to day activities.

Too often people do not identify the values that apply within groups that they are intending to mix with or that are inviting them to join. This should be done to compare the group's standards to your own values.

This comparison of values, most effectively done in a written form, should be an essential part of any new venture involving new associations of any sort.

Controlling aggression

We all get frustrated at different times at not having situations go the way we would like or not being able to control a situation or another person as we think we should be able to. This particularly can happen in situations with children who very often don't respond the way adults, particularly those with little experience I parenting, would like.

Very often the outcome of this frustration is a feeling of aggression. One of the keys to being successful in life is to be able to defuse this aggression and replace it with appropriate assertive behavior or, if all else fails, to get out of the situation for a time and return to it only when you are able to deal with it in a constructive manner.

The best technique for defusing or transforming the aggression is to form a picture clearly in your mind that the aggression is not focused on you, but is being projected from the other person in a random way and you just happen to be in the surrounding area. In this way, whether you have particular responsibility for the other person or do just happen to be an unrelated bystander you can formulate a strategy based on a planned intervention rather than an emotional defense of your ego.

Remember, if all else fails, provided you don't leave the other person open to an even worse outcome than if you stayed around, just get out of the situation and come back later.

Decide for yourself

Don't let other people decide what you are going to do. Part of being successful is being able to:

> *Decide that you want to stay with a job or activity that you do well and enjoy, and ensure that you are recognized for the contribution that you make.*

Similarly, standing by your beliefs and being respected for being honest with yourself and others about how you really feel is vital.

As an example, one of my staff was required to recruit a new person for a job and, despite writing a quite restrictive and demanding advertisement, he received in excess of 100 applications. He seemed concerned and I queried the reason.

He said that in speaking to the candidates, he found that many of them were in good positions already and were unable to say why they were seeking a change, other than for the money or just for the sake of a change.

This lack of a comprehensive assessment of a change strategy was quite foreign to my successful team member because he had always based a move on a thorough analysis of dissatisfaction with one job or extreme attraction to another.

The message is to not be driven to change by other people. Assess your situation and decide what you want to do. If you are happy don't let other people unsettle you. The grass is definitely not always greener on the other side of the fence.

Develop your own style

One thing that many people seem to forget is our uniqueness as human beings. I am still amazed by how many people still describe things as 'quite' unique or 'very' unique when the whole point of being unique is being the only one of a type.

You cannot be very or quite unique. You are unique, one of a kind. You should always remember that you are the only one of your type. You are as unique as your fingerprint.

The great thing is that this uniqueness extends well beyond your fingerprints and really should be a central part of the enjoyment of your life. In fact, I believe that a key part of personal success is realizing this uniqueness exists and developing it.

I am not suggesting a crazy egomaniacal shrine in your bedroom, but certainly a keen appreciation that you as a person are different from everyone else and have a unique contribution to make to the world is essential.

To be personally successful, you have to have this belief in your own uniqueness to help you establish an identity in a world that often seems crowded and can make you doubt your own significance and worth.

So think about it. You are the only you and realizing it, enjoying it and communicating with this in mind is an important part of personal success.

Peer group pressure

It is amazing how all of us are so bound by the limitations created by the opinions of others.

I had a case recently where I was seeking to assist a young person to break away from pre-conceived ideas other people had placed in her mind about what they saw as her limitations. After several sessions she started to look outside those supposedly limited areas and see a whole new world for herself. When she presented these new ideas to the people who were close to her, however, they said 'that's not you, you're not like that, you're more like this'.

This upset her quite significantly. This conflict between what she wanted to be and what people close to her wanted her to be caused her such stress that she went back to her old way of behaving and repeating in her mind the views that these other people had about her.

It is very difficult to find the true path to developing yourself without cutting off those who are important to you if they maintain a negative view of you and your life's journey.

Certainly, there are some horrendous stories about people who are lead astray by groups that promise to find them a new life. But one of the challenges for people who wish to be personally successful is finding out how to break away from those old habits that are sustained by the people who surround them, without falling prey to still worse circumstances.

The trick is to focus on the behaviors involved. 'Are they positive and productive? Do you see them as part of your continuing successful lifestyle?

Of so, you need to build on the behaviors that are already part of your successful lifestyle and eliminate those that contribute to lack of success. The people who align with these new behaviors will be obvious to you.

Don't accept false idols

In considering the issue of images that should be rejected because they provide poor brain food I was disappointed to speak to a young woman who had rejected a business career because of her knowledge of successful business people. She saw these people as poor role models and had negative feelings about how they achieved their success.

This woman still entered into a very worthwhile career, but I couldn't help but feel that her inability to reject these false idols may have contributed to her not pursuing a career which may have resulted in her contributing still more significantly to the community in a business sense.

It is very hard when working in a subordinate position in any education system to see past the false idols that are paraded before you and not to form negative images. Long term, however, it is important to understand that the rejection of these negative images and the control of your own input is an important part of the happiness in, happiness out formula.

Parents need to work with their children on the happiness in, happiness out formula to make sure that they can recognize these false idols and not let them contribute towards knee jerk reactions in relation to their own future. Happiness in, happiness out should mean a total blotting out of these people in terms of any influence on the activities of a young person, other as a symbol of what not to do..

The beauty of being young or new to the happiness in, happiness out formula is that the impact is just that much more dramatic and more enjoyable. Similarly, the double whammy of controlling that happiness in is even more dramatic for someone young or a newcomer to controlling inputs to their own emotions.

Don't invite danger

One of the strangest things about the uncontrolled, unpredictable garbage in, garbage out management of our own brains is how we so often invite other people to fill our heads with rubbish.

It seems that early on in everyone's life there develops a view that often becomes permanently ingrained, that intuition, independent thinking and personal confidence should run a long second to being taught things, working in a team or following the tried and true path.

So often I have found in doing assessments that the people who are really successful, particularly in establishing new ventures, are those who have a very high score on a measure of independent-mindedness.

These people don't need the approval of others for their own ideas. They don't necessarily reject other people's ideas but they don't feel a need to rely on other people and have their support in order to believe that what they're doing is worthwhile and will be a successful strategy either personally or in business.

So once again, the Happiness In, Happiness Out philosophy is a winner for those people who are independent-minded because they have a personality trait which says to them they don't need the opinion of others because their own thoughts are entirely adequate for their needs.

SUMMARY

These themes will help you draft your Personal Action List for this chapter:

INDEPENDENT-MINDEDNESS

- **Prize yourself worth.**
- **Know your own mind.**
- **Seek and accept good advice, not approval.**
- **Explain yourself only where appropriate.**

PERSONAL ACTION LIST
(Key words, actions & events to memorize, visualize and discuss)

Independent Behavior

_____

_____

_____

_____

_____

_____

_____

_____

_____

_____

_____

_____

_____

_____

_____

_____

_____

_____

_____

CHAPTER 8

COURAGEOUS BEHAVIOR

Courageous behavior is consistent with the fearless independence and sincerity that sustains a positive and intense approach to life.

Cowardly behavior is consistent with the fearful dependence and insincerity that sustains a negative and vague approach to life.

Definition: To be brave enough to do what you feel is right and develop the capacity to present and stand by a point of view.

The willingness and the courage to stand up for what you believe is right for you.

Statement: I know I have to do what is right.

Action:

- Do something practical you have been scared of doing.
- Stand up to someone who has tended to intimidate you.
- Start A positive/supportive conversation with a negative person you encounter.
- Declare your belief on a subject when you do not know the other persons point of view.

Ability to Cope with Adversity

In counseling a person experiencing difficulties recently it occurred to me again that the ability to cope with adversity is a key factor in being successful.

In this case, the individual was certainly under a lot of pressure but was seeking the widest possible range of alternatives to minimize the effect of the problems on himself and his family.

This ability to cope with adversity with a positive approach is not something that is just a function of a person's personality. You can use your goal-directed skills of visualizing your goals and writing down your strategies for achievement to cope with adverse circumstances.

In these situations it can be very difficult but you should aim to clear your mind of feelings of fear and panic to allow constructive thinking to prevail.

In very severe circumstances, it may be advisable to seek counseling or even medical intervention to allow you to relax, but the most important issue is that you try to remain in control of the circumstances and direct all of your activities toward a goal that is predetermined by you.

Even though at times your hold on the rudder may be shaky, success will come if you maintain the approach that has served you well in the good times.

Don't accept hypocrisy

It's a sad situation that there is so much hypocritical behavior in our society today. People who are on the road to success will certainly not accept this behavior as normal and will strive to work with people who are determined, able to practice what they preach and give credit where credit is due.

Over the years the development of a facade and the reaping of rewards in total disproportion to effort expended has become something of a well-developed frame of reference. However, genuine success, happiness and contentment comes from pursuing goals that are worthwhile on a level playing field.

It may seem old fashioned but the promotion of a reward system based on equity rather than the ability to generate success by playing the system should still in my view be a key part of true success.

This is where those who strive for success make long ranging personal ethical decisions that are only ever bought home to roost in one's own conscience.

Regrettably, different people's definition of conscience can make this an area of conjecture in its own right.

However, those who are honest with themselves will admit readily the merit or otherwise of their achievements.

Don't Be Angry About the Weaknesses of Others

In building your own happiness model, one of the most difficult things to do is to remain positive about the weaknesses of others.

All people have shortcomings and the closer we are to people, the more aware we will be of those shortcomings.

It is very easy to think of building your own happiness model by being angry and rejecting the perceived negative aspects of others, particularly those close to us, which result from their weaknesses. Parents especially can come in for quite a deal of negativity from their children because of parental weaknesses to which their children are exposed.

A positive approach to dealing with the possible negativity arising out of the weaknesses of one's parents, other family members or friends is to recognize only the true happiness components as providing any useful input to your own happiness.

Rather than fighting what you perceive to be the negative aspects, work with the happiness behaviors and let the negative emotions slide right on by.

Clearly, this isn't an easy task but purely as an exercise in trying to recognize behaviors and emotions that contribute to your happiness and those that do not, it is worth doing. Any contribution that this ability to select the positive behaviors can make to not becoming angry in a relationship is a bonus.

Relationship dynamics are always challenging. Applying the happiness in, happiness out philosophy that rejects dwelling on emotional negatives is a good strategy for maintaining the overall positive feeling in a relationship

Fight for your rights

It was emphasized to me so clearly once again in counseling someone who had been poorly treated by their employer that there comes a time you must stand up and fight for your rights.

It is all very well to go through life with a conciliatory and co-operative attitude, but one should never allow ones dignity and the welfare of one's family to be mercilessly trodden on.

In this case an employer had acted totally ruthlessly and inhumanely and attempted to smooth over the situation by virtually brainwashing the person involved.

It is very important in being personally successful to be aware that there are certain situations, hopefully not happening too often, where you do have to fight. Also when you do fight, do it with all your might and with all your personal skill and support systems.

It is rare for me to speak about total assertiveness, but it is a personal success strategy that must be kept in your armory for when it is necessary to battle with an aggressor who has no morals and can be dealt with in no other way.

A word of warning, don't let your standards slip by getting too close and acquiring some of the standards of your opponent.

Think and act smart but leave the dirty pool to the other side otherwise the path to personal success will become awfully slippery and unrewarding.

Keep to your standards

When you are bombarded with other people's opinions, both personally and in the media on a regular basis, it is very difficult to do one of the things that is most significant for being personally successful.

That is to set your own standards in relation to personal behavior and stick to them. Even after setting high standards for yourself it is so easy to compromise when you see other people taking it easy and working to a lower standard.

Developing and maintaining a class act has never been easy but this is what sets apart the people who are truly successful in life. You have to set your own standards and then maintain them in the face of a fairly heavy barrage of mediocrity.

Two ways of keeping the standard clearly in focus are to study the standards of people past and present that you admire and second to commit to writing down observable aspects of your personal standards that you can use to check your performance at any given time.

In this way you can form your own rules to help you keep up your personal standards rather than looking outward and being disappointed as you feel yourself slipping down as a result of negative external influences.

You won't be disappointed when you set your own rules and follow them.

Personal rules and integrity

One particular area that I believe is a problem for our community is a general lack of personal integrity. I believe that many people have not had the opportunity to develop skills for developing their own personal rules in this area.

Even with changing education systems placing greater emphasis on life skills, I believe the general core of developing rules for life and the principles that must be applied on a day-to-day basis for personal improvement and improvement of the community is still lacking.

It is sad that people are not made aware very early in their educational experience that developing core values that can give their life greatly added value is such a simple and pleasurable task.

As with everything, it is never too late to develop these skills. In essence, it only requires the most basic application of the following test.

Which of your behaviors are in the best interest of you, your immediate family and the community?

All of us answer these questions in different ways, but if we truly apply the values test it is amazing how the behaviors that result all meet a similar standard of civil behaviour. In addition, the resulting goal focus can carry us through to the development of a successful lifestyle and personal career achievement.

So, if you have not taken the time or had the opportunity thrust upon you, sit down and write down the values you live by and put them to the test.

Stick to your guns

One thing we all must learn to do if we want to be successful is to stick to our guns (figuratively speaking of course) and remain resolute when we know we are on a good thing and are developing a good idea.

There are just too many people around who will happily criticize what someone else puts forward even though they will never come forward with an idea of their own.

Sometimes it is a real battle to continue with your own ideas when these people are putting you down, but if you can stick with it the rewards can be enormous.

It is important of course to realize the difference between people having a go at you and picking on your ideas and those situations where people are constructively trying to help you.

A key attribute of people who would be successful is that they can pick the knockers from the genuine helpers and work with the genuine helpers whilst cutting the knockers right out of the system altogether.

So the strategies to be developed are:

- **Have faith in yourself and your ideas**

- **Work with people who will constructively criticize and help you develop your ideas**

- **Ignore the destructive people who have no interest in success whether it is yours or their own**.

SUMMARY

These themes will help you draft your Personal Action List for this chapter:

COURAGEOUS BEHAVIOUR

- **Focus.**
- **Don't delay the inevitable.**
- **Consider the penalties not the emotions.**
- **Have faith in yourself.**

(Key words, actions & events to memorize, visualize and discuss)

Courageous

_____
_____
_____
_____
_____
_____
_____
_____
_____
_____

CHAPTER 9

Sincere Behavior

Sincerity is the essence of personal success because of the feeling of fulfillment it gives you and the power that it injects into your actions.

Insincerity is the essence of failure because of the feeling of hollowness it leaves in you and the shallowness that it injects into your actions.

Definition: Free from pretence or deceit with yourself and others in feelings, manner or actions.
Belief in your ideas and their worth.

Statement: Sharing my positive thoughts feels great.

Action:

- Write down the things in your life which mean most to you.
- Write down your complete philosophy of life in a formal statement.
- Explain your thoughts on life to someone else.
- Write down why your philosophy of life makes life worthwhile.

Introduction

The essential element in the quest for interpersonal success is the personal mission statement in which you make it clear to yourself and others why you do what you do. It is the spiritual element of your strategy. It is the process that gives you inner peace and long term strength. The following strategies are just some I have thought of over the years. Do not hesitate to add your own to make your success truly personal.

What does it mean?

Because I speak about integrity so often as an essential part of personal success, people often ask me what I mean exactly by integrity.

Very simply, I answer that integrity is all about honesty, being honest with yourself and being honest with others.

There is an old saying in relation to entertainment that you should never let the facts get in the way of a good story. In other words, in telling a joke, embellishment is an essential part of being successful.

That may be OK for joke telling, but in the business of real life it's the people who don't let the facts get in the way of a good story who are those who lack integrity.

It's very simple really. Integrity means don't be careless with the truth. Learn to face up to the bad news about yourself and others, rather than changing the facts to fit the circumstances. Also, don't pretend that you don't realize that society has rules that are as plain as the nose on everybody's face and are there for the basic business of being fair.

Follow these very simple rules and you will be perceived as someone who is achieving personal success with integrity as a key element in your personal style.

Be cordial

Having an encounter with a service technician very recently made me realize once again the importance of maintaining a cordial approach in any of your dealings with other people.

This particular person was clearly not comfortable with his role and when difficulties arose moved quickly to be defensive and to attack others verbally when it was just not appropriate.

To be cordial does not mean to be subservient. It means to remain polite no matter how emphatically you may need to present an argument, even on safety and other life and death issues. Indeed, the cordiality associated with maintaining a level head can be just that much more dramatic in its impact when contrasted with the possibly very powerful message that is being delivered.

The people that I recall from my experience who had a real personal impact were able to keep their cool, never lost respect for the other person and practiced cordiality even when the circumstances were grim and the solutions being implemented were harsh.

Opinions in this area will differ, but my view is that emotionality resulting in verbal abuse or any other nasty behavior is just not appropriate and not at all associated with individual personal success.

Be genuine (i)

I recall vividly having my first meeting with the Chief Executive of a very large organization who was most frustrated in his dealings with his Senior Executives.

This Chief Executive just could not understand why so many of the Senior Executives who worked for him insisted on constantly telling him what they thought he wanted to hear. He genuinely wanted them to give their own opinion about the issues that were discussed and he paid them very high salaries to come to grips with problems and recommend solutions.

Instead of getting his team's honest opinions, this CEO suffered constant games of people trying to second guess what he would like them to say and what his own answer would be if he were doing their job.

Lacking the self confidence in their own ability to make decisions and analyze problems, the team resorted to trying to avoid failure and criticism by developing a situation where they would at least be perceived as agreeing or being subservient to their leader.

This type of behavior is unfortunately very common and results in a stifling of the career progression of many people. The extent to which it is negative emotionally for the particular person differs greatly. In almost all the cases I have experienced, whether the person stays in the situation or removes themselves, they normally have a frustrating and unhappy existence.

A key behavior for being successful is to develop the ability to relate to other people on a one on one level based on very positive views that you must have about your own self esteem and self confidence, and theirs.

Be genuine (ii)

There seems to be a continuing unfortunate modern trend based on the philosophy that you can fool some of the people all of the time and all of the people some of the time. It seems that a firm belief has been developed by many people that as long as you are busy doing either of these two things then you are a smart operator who will survive long enough to make some money.

There are numerous cases which reinforce this view, but it does not mean that the people who follow these philosophies are personally successful.

I believe it is the general acceptance of the philosophy that we are all going to be fooled sometime that allows us to ignore, forgive or just tolerate so many things that we really don't agree with. This exaggerated example of the live and let live philosophy means that we really don't get involved when people make outrageous claims, do outrageous things or do things that harm others.

One should differentiate between people who do their best, fail, admit it and get on with trying again and those who totally stuff up, make a million excuses and continue stuffing up and blaming their failures on others. The truly successful person will help the hard worker do better and be totally unforgiving of the hopeless excuses given by the non performer.

Be trustworthy

One of the most important attributes for achieving personal success is trustworthiness.

Defining trustworthiness is not as easy as it might seem at first appearance, but if we think about a person that you know and trust the concept becomes much clearer. Furthermore, if you relate it to your own image it certainly gives you something to work towards.

For people to say that someone can be trusted is generally perceived as being a major compliment. To achieve such a compliment requires a significant commitment to respecting the interests of another in every possible way. Being trustworthy doesn't just happen, it is a developed characteristic.

People who have the capacity to protect the interests of others, especially by not abusing personal information about them or taking advantage of their general personal vulnerability in any way will have the pleasure of being regarded as trustworthy.

Unfortunately it is just so easy to stray from the path of trust. Fortunately, one of the beauties of this particular characteristic is that it is personally rewarding in its own right and those who practice it will need no confirmation of their self worth because they value trust in themselves and others.

Cherish the family

It is not unusual for me to encounter people who are in difficult circumstances. It is at these times that I am able to emphasize just how important the family is in relation to overall self-esteem, personal security and general success.

One thing that I emphasize most strongly for people with doubt about their own worth is the need to cherish the family. The family can take on many different connotations for people, but essentially it is about the people who you may live with on a day to day basis, who care where you are, what you are doing and to whom you turn when life's adventures become challenging.

These are the people who matter and whose acceptance is critical for your psychological well being. It is their support that will see you through the difficult times. Also, by giving them support you build a strong, mutually-fulfilling relationship which is the centre piece of your life.

So if you want to be personally successful, develop a clear perspective of those relationships that form the vocal point of your life, and don't allow yourself to be distracted and distorted by the wider group, who, as I say on so many occasions really just don't care.

Look to the family, which is where you will find the opinions and feelings that really matter.

Consider other people's feelings

I have heard it said that to take too much of account of other people's feelings is a sign of weakness. I believe this is absolutely incorrect and that to have a consideration for other people's feelings is a sign of personal strength. It is also a sign of great perception and the capacity to use knowledge of how other people's emotions work to bring about the best possible result for everyone that you are involved with.

So often people feel that success is all about marching over the top of people and somehow applying the philosophy of the survival of the fittest to every circumstance they encounter.

To be successful is to be successful as a person and a person is someone who respects the feelings of others no matter who they may be. So if you wish to be truly successful, develop skills in understanding how you impact on others and consider the feelings of others in what you do.

In most cases there will be an immediate reward in seeing personal development in others that will be sufficient for you to know that you have managed the circumstances in a professional and humane way.

More importantly you will feel personally rewarded at the development and application of a vital people skill.

Value your friends

One thing that seems to be a problem these days with the 'hub-bub' created by hi-tech communication is the establishment and maintenance of really good friendships.

High technology and information overload seems to have had a destabilizing effect on many people's emotions, particularly loyalty. Being pushed from pillar to post by numerous media influences seems to have made people more prone to doubting loyalty even amongst their best friends.

One of the hallmarks of true friendship is unquestioning loyalty.

While unquestioning obedience is always potentially dangerous, unquestioning loyalty is not so. Loyalty is not blind, but it certainly isn't fickle. It is one of the essential ingredients in building working and social relationships that help successful people establish and progress a secure and positive lifestyle.

Think carefully about the people that you are totally loyal to and to whom you could honestly say you have an unshakeable attitude of positive support. You may well be disappointed at how few there are.

The good part of developing unquestioning loyalty is that once the skills have been established in one or two relationships it seems easier to determine situations where loyalty is warranted and to expand the loyal network of friends that is so vital to overall success.

Don't brow beat people

In listening to the newly appointed Chief Executive of a business organization introduce himself recently at a meeting; I was astounded at how this senior person had no concept of how to present himself subtly to the audience.

In circumstances which required finesse and feeling, but forthrightness, he got the whole thing back to front.

His delivery was extremely forthright, had absolutely no finesse and took no account of the audience's feelings. Around me I could see people wishing him off the stage and cringing at style of presentation. Clearly, this person had not done his research and bombed out as a result.

If you have to make a presentation make sure you understand what your role is in the situation and prepare accordingly. Be aware of the audience's needs and feelings and make the presentation appropriate for the audience.

Nobody likes to be thumped into submission even when the circumstances may suggest that this technique has a part to play. If the best technique is one of subtlety, on the other hand, and a bashing is delivered, the situation deteriorates into being almost laughable.

So pick the style to suit the occasion and you will be a winner every time. On the other hand, if you do not know your audience, you stand a very good chance of being a monumental flop.

Don't ignore the silent types

In doing a major survey of employees in an organization recently, I had the great pleasure of meeting the classic Australian quiet achiever.

This lady had worked for the organization for many years and risen to a position of quite some responsibility. The significant thing about this particular person was her apparent lack of ambition. She certainly had not aspired to be in charge of her work area and had no aspirations for further promotion. Interestingly, she had been given a profit share of this substantial business without even indicating any interest in being rewarded in that way.

It is important to realize that these quiet achievers do exist. It is a great regret to me that I often find them in organizations, but being totally ignored and under-valued. If they are undervalued they do not wait around working for people who do not merit their respect. Many organizations lose valuable people without even realizing that they have existed.

Successful people are aware of the existence of these quiet achievers, work closely with them and share their success.

So if you encounter quieter people, do not assume that quietness relates to lack of ability or enthusiasm. Quite the opposite can be true. Truly successful people see value in people well beyond their superficial characteristics.

Setting an example

Recently a friend gave me a tremendous example of the impact of one very important strategy for personal success, which is, setting a good example.

Apparently, he had been on a rain forest walk and on the way back had noticed an empty plastic drink container lying beside the track. Quite unobtrusively he had picked up the container and stored it in his bag and disposed of it later in a waste bin.

Unbeknown to him, he had been observed by a younger member of the group who shortly after, somewhat conspicuously, identified a piece of waste along the track, picked it up and took it along to a bin further on.

My friend went out of his way to compliment this young person in relation to his responsible attitude to the environment. He told me later about the incident as an example of how much impact setting a good example can have in releasing the normally inhibited behavior of others in relation to socially responsible activities.

A keen awareness of the 'do as I do' thinking that influences not just young people but the general community is a key factor for personal success. Successful people realize that nothing they do goes unobserved and any negative things have the potential to cause deterioration in general community standards and, conversely, any positive things they do have an equal capacity to influence things in a positive way.

Don't just take or just give

We are all familiar with the expression give and take. Certainly in relationships, in everyday life and in the work situation, give and take has a central part to play.

Those who would be successful realize that to give in any of these relationships is absolutely essential. On the other hand, they also realize that being alert for the other person just taking rather than giving receiving can create problems.

It's often a fine line, but that difference between the other person receiving what you give or taking from you, however willing you might be, is the beginning of the end for many relationships.

To be successful it is essential to make it clear to people that, while you give and are happy to see people receive, being taken is not on your agenda.

When people realize that you are not going to be a doormat, they will either respect you more and stop taking from you or they will go elsewhere so they can find a doormat that they can walk on and continue their selfish behavior.

If you want to be successful you'll be one of the people who sets the guidelines very clearly, and very early, that while you give and like to see people receive you will not be the victim of another person's selfishness.

Empathy

Empathy is the ability to appreciate another person's feelings without becoming so emotionally involved that your judgment is impaired. It sharpens our perception in all sorts of situations in our daily lives and work. It helps us to increase our understanding and enjoyment of other people. It is a state of mind which anyone can develop and improve.

We can acquire empathy through role-playing. One of the biggest mistakes we make in dealing with others is to underestimate the importance of their feelings. To grasp the essential feeling-pattern of another person, try to put yourself in their shoes.

The first step in this process is to find out what they are like. We cannot assume that others feel exactly as we do when faced with a situation. Empathy requires you to forget your own reactions and attempt to see the world through the eyes of the other person.

All of us practice empathy at times without knowing it. Developing meaningful relationships with others would be difficult without it. The trick is to learn to apply this approach consciously and deliberately. There is little we cannot learn about others if we can tune in to the feelings and thoughts behind their words and actions.

In addition, this awareness of how others think and feel can be the key to effective leadership and management, as well as improving general interpersonal relations.

So put yourself in the other person's position. You will find it a good starting point to developing empathy.

Forget swings and roundabouts

A lot of people who are unjustly dealt with comfort themselves by thinking that the person will have their day in court so to speak.
My finding is that not only is this not the case very often, but to live with this belief to somehow rationalize a bad experience is very negative.

Having a firm grasp on the realities of life and maintaining a personal philosophy based on dealing with things positively and in a controlled way is much more appropriate for achieving personal success than believing that the bad people of the world will get their due.

It is much more appropriate to work on the principle that you will be recognized for your own achievements rather than believing that some mysterious process of natural justice will even out the experiences of life.

People who are going to be personally successful will attribute success or otherwise to their own activities and will lay any blame for failure firmly at their own door.

A very old adage (the Serenity Prayer) says basically that it is very wise to change the things that you are capable of changing, accept those that you cannot change and make sure you know the difference.[8]

It is certainly much more productive to focus your efforts on the areas where you can take control and make the necessary changes. Those who would achieve personal success would certainly have this focus.

---

[8] The Serenity Prayer (common name) attributed to Reinhold Niebuhr (1892–1971).

Fulfill your obligations

It is amazing just how much of a negative impact one small incident of unreliability can have on your profile. One key to being personally successful is to develop a reputation for fulfilling your obligations.

If people are relying on you, don't let them down. Make sure that you don't make commitments that you are not going to meet.

It is far better to say no and not get involved than to over commit yourself and find that you are constantly letting people down. Your reputation will soon suffer and quite correctly because you have embarrassed people and caused them inconvenience purely through your own lack of consideration.

So think about how much time you have available and your capabilities, then only commit yourself to obligations that you know you can fulfill.

Conversely, keep a balance and don't let yourself become a slave to others by volunteering to do everything for everyone.

You will soon fall by the wayside if you try to do the impossible. So do what you can, do it well and all will be well.

Get in touch with your feelings

It strikes me that many people have a problem with acknowledging their inner most feelings. Experiencing the feelings of fear, even dread, turmoil, jealousy, passion, boredom and so on is a basic part of life.

Too often people have been told that they should deny the existence of these innermost feelings, because being stable, disciplined and well organized is being normal.

Certainly, reacting anti-socially to any of these intense feelings is something that our society has decided is not acceptable, but this does not mean that we should deny that these feelings exist. On the contrary, suppressing them can lead to anti-social reactions due to frustration.

It is much more constructive to acknowledge these feelings, accept them as normal and share them with those around us.

Getting in touch with, and fully understanding, your feelings is an essential part of achieving personal success in life.

Those who would be successful not only get closely in touch with their own feelings but are able to help others who may not have the skill.

Give of yourself

One of the things I have observed in people who are truly successful is their willingness and capacity to contribute freely to the welfare of others.

People who are successful are not normally selfish and do not keep their success strategies to themselves. They share them with those who are genuinely interested and have the same values.

Similarly, they normally are very open about what their approach has been and give freely of their time to people who want to know how they have achieved success.

This does not mean that they allow all sorts of people to waste their time. But in circumstances where it is appropriate they are happy to speak about their strategies. Usually this is with people who they see are already making a very sustained effort and are on the right track.

Conversely, they usually have little time for people who are looking for the easy way out and are not prepared to do any of the hard work.

One of the benefits of being willing to share ideas with people who have similar goals is that you almost invariably learn as much from them as they learn from you.

So when you are on that path to success don't shun other people who are working for the same goals, take time to share ideas, you will find that the benefit is a mutual one.

Giving compliments

An interesting area in life is the giving and receiving of compliments. Accepting compliments gracefully is an acquired skill. Equally, developing the art of proficiently delivering a compliment is important and requires sincerity and inspiration.

A genuine, appreciative remark helps to reinforce our inherent self-worth (both of the giver and receiver) and is one of the best ways to develop good relations with other people.

The art of paying a compliment takes thought and practice. Many of us have experienced the discomfort of having a compliment fall through because we chose the wrong time or the wrong words in which to phrase it. Choosing the right approach is just as important as choosing the right words.

Interestingly, compliments are often offered publicly in a light-hearted fashion so they can be accepted without making demands of the recipient, who can laugh along with the crowd and happily accept the tribute. More formal compliments are more powerful and the skill of speaking sincerely in tribute of another human being is a key skill for being successful.

Compliments well given and well received deepen social relationships, help to boost the egos of both parties and encourage us to new achievements. Compliments are a powerful force for good will and a natural gesture used in the daily interactions of business people. They should be a natural part of daily life, but this requires a better and more mature understanding of people that only comes with practice.

Have a General Liking for People

Working recently with someone who showed great care in his dealings with all people in his organization reminded me yet again of the importance of a caring attitude.

This person was particularly focused and achieved his time and quality goals on a very large project although many areas where he was dependent on others could have resulted in failure.

Rather than being aggressive and pushing other people into achieving their goals, this business owner worked in a very caring way, got the best out of the people involved and organized a successful team effort.

When things get difficult, there is often a temptation to become aggressive and to try to pressure others into achieving goals that you think are the right ones. While this may work in the short term, it is very debilitating for the individual and the team in the medium and long term.

Striking a balance between achieving the immediate goal and developing the team for future challenges is an ability that needs to be developed and requires a caring attitude.

One of the key factors in developing this style and incorporating it into your Personal Success Strategies is to have a positive feeling about the work of others and allowing them to use their strengths. Focusing on a team member's inevitable weaknesses is a sure way to de-motivate that person and the team.

If you develop the skill of working with people's strengths, you'll find success in the short, medium and long term. It is amazing how a combination of team strengths can make all of the teams' weakness seem that much more manageable.

Respect the achievements & efforts of others

Inevitably, people who are truly personally successful will be those who genuinely respect the achievements and efforts of others in the community, no matter what level of influence or public recognition these people may have achieved.

To me this is because people who respect these efforts and achievements have an inner quality of empathy that allows them to be just that much more in touch with the world around them and the people that they deal with.

This quality of empathy is one that is essential for personal success. To cruise or crash through life, treading on other people and pushing other people out of the way has nothing whatever to do with personal success.

True personal success comes from working with people, enjoying that interaction and contributing to the success and fulfillment of others.

So look around you and see if you are able to appreciate what other people are contributing and achieving. It can be a most illuminating test as to whether or not you have an outward directed strategy that is consistent with personal success.

If you are selfishly inwardly directed , you may find that you are locked into a strategy of personal aggrandizement rather than real personal success that .involves giving.

Once you have completed Personal Success Strategies, a whole new world opens up. The world of helping others is where personal success truly comes into your life.

Help others

There have been numerous stories over the centuries about the benefits of being charitable. I don't believe that there has been any change in this situation. Taking the opportunity to help someone else, in whatever way, benefits not only the receiver but the giver.

There is a natural and positive part of our personality that allows us to benefit greatly from sharing with others. Whether it be our personal wealth, our knowledge or our personal energies in working with others on a charitable cause, the process of giving has the capacity to enrich an individual's existence quite dramatically.

It is not just the feeling of helping that brings personal reward. Inevitably these activities allow you to relate to people who are similarly motivated. This feeling of camaraderie adds greatly to the basic experience of giving.

Those people who are truly successful know that the process of sharing brings them that much closer to a situation of fulfillment, happiness and completeness. It is probably the one true indicator of our humanity.

So when the opportunity arises don't hold back, give, in the knowledge that it is a natural and basic part of a successful lifestyle.

It's a moral thing

It was fascinating to see a friend who I greatly admire get most excited in a discussion recently when we spoke about whether a person's talent could make up for them being a person of doubtful morals.

My friend was adamant that there was no way that he would ever accept that great skill in business management for example, could make up for someone taking advantage of those who are less privileged.

It certainly reinforced my long held view that being successful and talented does not entitle a person to be beyond the law.

On the contrary, I believe that being successful is incompatible with any form of exploitive behavior.

In pursuing personal success some people do lose the plot but more often than not, the unacceptable behavior is unrelated to their skill development.

In my view, striving for personal success goes beyond developing your own high standards. It also involves setting a good example for others. So quite apart from disapproving of the unacceptable exploitive behavior those who would be truly personally successful accept responsibility for showing others the way. I see this as very much a part of my earnest friend's undisputed personal success.

Thoughtfulness

A pet hate of mine is people who drive along the road throwing small bits of rubbish out the window, particularly cigarette butts and cigarette packets.

Whoever coined the term, think globally act locally was really onto a good thing. Just as large corporations have a responsibility to the community, successful individuals are aware of their place in the community and treat their environment with respect, both physically and philosophically.

The littering example is just one pointed way of trying to show how habits can develop that form part of the bigger picture of not succeeding as a responsible member of the community. Sadly, it extends much more broadly into the treatment of one's neighbors, the relationship with one's family and all areas where the core of community commitment is tested.

This is an extremely interesting and important area because the irresponsible things are not necessarily illegal, but they are still negative. This leaves the decision squarely in the hands of the individual, as to where they place their interests compared to the interest of others around them.

An interesting test is to consider in the original example how you would feel if someone constantly threw cigarette butts, or empty cigarette packets, into your backyard. I think you would see your perspective change dramatically.

Try to keep hypocrisy to a minimum

All of us are hypocrites at times and don't live by the rules that we preach. It does not mean that we cannot attempt to live by a philosophy whereby we try to minimize our hypocrisy.

Being a straight shooter and living by the rules can be a tall order at times but is definitely a worthwhile goal.

The next time you are on your soap box and preaching about a particular situation, try to be realistic in your assessment of your own behavior in this area. You may surprise yourself with your limited credibility.

A very telling test is to think of someone else who has done exactly the same things as you have done and think carefully about what opinion you have of them. This may give you quite a fright.

We all have a blind spot about ourselves, but we can work to make it smaller. Personal revelations about our behavior may not have a major impact on our feelings immediately, but it can lead to much improved relations with others and then reflect back on our behavior.

The end result of developing self awareness of our hypocrisy can be a more honest and effective communicative style and a good start to a better style

Have a vision for life

So many people think that having a mission in life, or a personal vision, is the realm of one in a million people. On the contrary, it is something we all do and we all have.
Unfortunately, many of us miss out on the real pleasure of working with our visions and our achievements because we overlook how important they are in our life.

Don't be embarrassed about your visions, luxuriate in them. A good way to start, of course, is to commit them to writing and get them more finally tuned. After you have firmed up your plans, you can share them with your family and your friends and test out their reaction to find out how likely they are to be allies in your quest.

The final part of success in having a formal vision of life and achievement is to identify those people who accept that having a personal vision is a positive thing. This is because they will want to work with you because they have similar views and are looking to communicate with someone else who is interested in achievement.

Although this all sounds really simple, don't be surprised to strike the odd person who thinks you're a little bit strange, because many people have been educated to be reactive rather than pro-active in life. You may choose to take on the challenge of stimulating the interest of others who have not been involved in personal achievement planning. Alternatively, you may find it more your style to only work with people with similar views to your own.

Whatever you choose to do, don't lose your own thoughts about the fact that having a life's vision about what you would like to achieve in this life is a major personal success strategy.

SUMMARY

These themes will help you draft your Personal Action List for this chapter:

SINCERE BEHAVIOUR

- **Live by your clearly defined personal philosophy.**
- **Act without malice.**
- **Say what you feel.**
- **Consider the feelings of others.**

Personal Action List
(Key words, actions & events to memorize, visualize and discuss)

Sincere Behaviors I would like to develop

_____
_____
_____
_____
_____
_____
_____
_____
_____
_____
_____
_____
_____
_____
_____
_____
_____

Chapter 10

Conclusion

The challenge with developing any new human behavior is making it into a standard part of your lifestyle – your successful lifestyle. While habits are good and many books have been written about habits, I think this type of thinking promotes a less flexible approach to positive behaviors than the use of the word strategies.

Strategies are 'bigger', deeper and more flexible than habits.

You need to review and revise strategies regularly.

Habits make you think you have finished the job.

Strategies make you realize that only part of the journey is being managed and that this is the most rewarding aspect of a successful life – it is constantly evolving.

Now that you have considered each of the behaviors in the Personal Success Strategies Psychoframe, and seen examples of how they are applied, it is a good time to look at the basic principles and associated strategies as one concept.

This is a revision of all that has been presented in previous chapters and forms the basis of bringing the Psychoframe together in one strategy for managing your successful life.

When working with the various dimensions in the Psychoframe, it is important to realize that you can learn and think of them in the order they are presented in the PSQ and in the book, but life does not follow that order.

You have to be flexible about how the various parts of the Psychoframe can help you. It is just a social learning technique. You are the driver of how, where and when you use what it has taught you.

Here are the basic principles again. Do your best to relate them to what you do as well as what you think.

THE BASIC PRINCIPLES OF ACHIEVING PERSONAL SUCCESS

Positive behavior gives the pleasure of discharging stored energy through achievement, and achievement leaves you with an after taste of satisfaction and self-respect.

Intense behavior, driven by positive thoughts, brings issues closer, removes ignorance, reduces fear and increases the capacity to act.

Independent-mindedness confirms you as the focus of decision making, which makes you personally secure, able to stand firm and reject negative influences, leaving you feeling positive, powerful, satisfied and secure.

Courageous behavior is consistent with the fearless independence and sincerity that sustains a positive and intense approach to life.

Sincerity is the essence of personal success because of the feeling of fulfillment it gives you and the power that it injects into your actions.

REMEMBER, YOU NEED TO PRACTICE THE FOLLOWING ACTIONS

- **Always think positive.**

- **Live each moment to the full.**

- **Make up your own mind.**

- **Eliminate fear of fear itself.**

- **Know and say why you do what you do.**

Making these strategies part of your successful life

Using visualization to teach aspects of goal achievement made me aware many years ago that there is so much in the mind that stops us achieving what we want. Breaking free from that restrictive thinking is what Personal Success Strategies is all about. The examples I have given you are designed to show as many angles to this basic principle as possible.

In the final analysis, the real aim is for you to write your own success story. Even changing one thing about yourself can be the catalyst for a lifetime of change. I recall working with one very talented young woman who had only one basic personality element standing between her desires and their achievement. I could give her all the coaching in the world and try to give her the understanding she needed, but she had to internalize the need for change to get what she wanted.

In using this book, you have to do exactly the same thing. Learn the principles and practice the behavior that stands between you and what you define as success. It is amazing that so much of what we do not achieve is the result of our own inaction. Defining the action, applying the necessary principles and living your life the way you want starts in the mind, but quickly transfers to your life if you do it with enough commitment.

Good luck.

Annex

The Personal Review Form, below, allows you to set the guidelines within which you will use Personal Success Strategies to achieve what you want out of life.

PERSONAL REVIEW FORM (PRF)

Name: _____ **Date:** _____

PERSONAL DEVELOPMENT

Question: What areas of your life do you want to improve?

Answer:

_____
_____
_____
_____
_____
_____
_____
_____
_____

PERSONAL HISTORY

Question: How long have you been working on the personal development issues that are the greatest challenge for you?

Answer:

_____

Question: What have you done up to now to achieve your personal development goals?

Answer:_____

_____

_____

_____

_____

_____

_____

_____

ACHIEVEMENT EXPECTATIONS

Question: How long do you expect it will take before you start to make satisfactory progress on the achievement of you personal development goals? What are the biggest influences in this area?

Answer:

_____

_____

_____

_____

_____

_____

_____

_____

_____

_____

_____

_____

_____

DEVELOPMENT STRATEGY

Question: What current plans or ideas do you think are most likely to help you achieve your personal development goals?

Answer:

_____

_____

_____

_____

_____

_____

CRITICAL FACTORS

List all the information that you think is relevant to the achievement of your personal development goals. (How problems arose etc).

_____

_____

_____

_____

_____

_____

_____

_____

_____

_____

_____

_____

_____

_____

_____

_____

_____

_____

PERSONAL SUCCESS QUESTIONNAIRE (PSQ)

Name: _____**Date:** _____

INSTRUCTIONS

The PSQ is designed to help you learn more about your approach to personal challenges. It is open-ended and requires written answers.

The PSQ contains a series of statements followed by a space for you to write your response. You are required to respond as if you were speaking to someone who may make a statement or ask a question. Your response should be about **your** own attitudes, beliefs and experiences. You should not respond with a question.

Do not worry if you have no experience in this area. The PSQ uses no special jargon or other expressions which would be unfamiliar to you. Alternatively, although the questions are intended to be general, you may feel happier answering in relation to a particular situation you have experienced. Feel free to use any method of approach. The aim is to allow you to give your views on a variety of issues by simulating a discussion.

HERE IS A SAMPLE OF WHAT YOU WILL BE REQUIRED TO DO

Statement: Personal development training seems so vague.

Response: Not if I deal in specifics and practice key behaviors.

You may write as much as you like in the space provided, but you need to make **only two** different points to complete the item and achieve the maximum score.

The PSQ is completed with a time limit because the situations which are simulated are usually done under pressure with no opportunity to correct errors made.

You will have 30 minutes to do as many of the questions as possible. Work **quickly** but not so fast that you make mistakes. Ask any questions before you begin.

PLEASE TURN OVER AND START WORK

PSQ ITEMS

1.   Statement: How are you feeling today?

    Response:

_____

_____

2.   Statement: I just can't seem to get enthusiastic about anything.

    Response:

_____

_____

3.   Statement: What is independent thinking about anyway?

    Response:

_____

_____

4.   Statement: What is courage?

    Response:

_____

_____

5.   Statement: What is sincerity?

    Response:

_____

_____

6.   Statement: Do you get depressed sometimes?

      Response:

_____

_____

7.   Statement: Does being intense about things tire you out?

      Response:

_____

_____

8.   Statement: Does being independent-minded mean you are a loner?

      Response:

_____

_____

9.   Statement: How is courage relevant to personal success?

      Response:

_____

_____

10.   Statement: Why will people accept what I say?

      Response:

_____

_____

11.   Statement: You can't help feeling bad, if everyone around you feels bad!.

     Response:

_____

_____

12.   Statement: I don't like to get involved.

     Response:

_____

_____

13.   Statement: So what do I get out of developing independent-mindedness?

     Response:

_____

_____

14.   Statement: How do I learn to be courageous?

     Response:

_____

_____

15.   Statement: What is the key to success in personal relationships?

     Response:

_____

_____

16.　Statement:　Negative people are more powerful than positive people.

　　　Response:

_____

_____

17.　Statement:　Being intense just isn't me!

　　　Response:

_____

_____

18.　Statement:　Does being independent-minded mean you rebel against everything?

　　　Response:

_____

_____

19.　Statement:　How do I face someone that I've always been scared of?

　　　Response:

_____

_____

20.　Statement:　Isn't being genuine a bit of a weak strategy?

　　　Response:

_____

_____

21. Statement: It's easier to be negative than positive!

Response:

_____

_____

22. Statement: What's the point of getting passionate about things?

Response:

_____

_____

23. Statement: How do I know if I'm independent-minded?

Response:

_____

_____

24. Statement: Does success behavior get easier?

Response:

_____

_____

25. Statement: I'd rather just keep people at a distance!

Response:

_____

_____

PERSONAL ACTION LIST
(Key words, actions & events to memorize, visualize and discuss)

Positive

_____
_____
_____
_____
_____
_____
_____
_____

Intense

_____
_____
_____
_____
_____
_____
_____
_____

Independent-minded

_____
_____
_____
_____
_____
_____
_____
_____
_____

Courageous

_____
_____
_____
_____
_____
_____
_____
_____
_____

Sincere

_____
_____
_____
_____
_____
_____
_____
_____

Additional Notes

_____
_____
_____
_____
_____
_____
_____
_____
_____
_____
_____
_____
_____

INDEX

Final notes for my personal success plan

www.ingramcontent.com/pod-product-compliance
Lightning Source LLC
Chambersburg PA
CBHW071536040426
42452CB00008B/1041